HABITS OF THE MIND

HABITS OF THE MIND

TEN EXERCISES TO RENEW YOUR THINKING

Dr. Archibald D. Hart

WORD PUBLISHING
Dallas•London•Vancouver•Melbourne

Unless otherwise indicated, Scripture quotations used in this book are
from the King James Version of the Bible. Other quotations are from:

The Living Bible (TLB), copyright © 1971 by Tyndale House Publishers,
Wheaton, Ill. Used by permission.

The New English Bible (NEB). Copyright © 1961, 1970 by The Delegates
of the Oxford University Press and the Syndics of the Cambridge
University Press. Reprinted by permission.

Anecdotes and case studies included in this volume are based on actual
cases or are composites of actual cases. Names and details have been
changed to protect identities.

Library of Congress Cataloging–in–Publication Data
Hart, Archibald D.
    Habits of the mind : ten exercises to renew your thinking /
Archibald D. Hart.
       p.   cm.
    ISBN 0-8499-1219-9
    1. Success—Religious aspects—Christianity.   2. Happiness—
Religious aspects—Christianity.   3. Spiritual exercises.   I. Title.
BV4598.H37   1996
248.4—dc20

                                                                96–16040
                                                                    CIP

Printed in the United States of America
6 7 8 0 1 2 3 4 9 BVG 9 8 7 6 5 4 3 2 1

To the memory of
RICHARD ALAN MORRIS
our son-in-law and husband of our daughter Sharon,
who tragically died on March 21, 1995.

And also to his two sons, our grandsons,
VINCENT MORRIS and ALAN MORRIS.

CONTENTS

Once again I am indebted to many for helping me to bring this project to completion:

To my wonderful wife, Kathleen, for her support and encouragement throughout this project, especially since it was undertaken during a period of personal grief for all our family. She continues to teach me how to be a healthy thinker in many, many ways.

To the Board of Trustees of Fuller Theological Seminary and President Richard Mouw for granting me a sabbatical so that I could undertake this and several other tasks.

To my colleagues in the Graduate School of Psychology who have tolerated my leadership for the past thirteen years and given me enough freedom to develop my writing and other skills. I value, more than anything else, your collegiality and esteem. It hasn't always been deserved, but it has been my mainstay for many years.

To the rest of my family, especially my daughter, Sharon, for your loving support during these past six months of tragedy and adjustment. I am never sure whether it has been the best of times or the worst of times, but it certainly has transformed us for the better. And for this I give thanks to God.

More than with any of my other books, I gave a lot of thought about what to call this one. It seems fashionable these days to do everything by "sevens." The "Seven Habits of Almost Anything" seems to be a formula for many popular books, addressing topics ranging from happiness to excellence.

So, in considering a title, I must confess I did consider calling this volume, *The Seven Habits of a Healthy Mind.* However, the temptation only lasted about ten seconds. Yes, seven is a very convenient number—it seems so perfect, even biblical, like the seven days of creation in Genesis or the seven seals of Revelation.

But "Seven Habits" was too arbitrary. And it forced me to leave out a couple of very important habits. Consequently, I have settled on "Ten Habits." I need to stress, however, that by limiting myself to a discussion of the ten most important habits that characterize a healthy mind, I am not suggesting that these are the only ones to be considered.

The ten habits that form the core of my book are those I have most frequently found in friends and clients whom I consider to be happy and successful people. I believe they are important to both mental and spiritual health. There may well be other habits that you need to consider for yourself. If so, my ten will help to illustrate how you should develop your own healthy habits. As for the concept of "habits," there is no better word to describe precisely what I want to talk about— the thought habits that make up a healthy mind.

I have also given a lot of consideration to how I can help you, the reader, benefit from the practical advice I offer. Because the topic is so important, I ask you to make a pact with me, to follow through on all the exercises I recommend. To benefit from this book, you'll need to practice every habit and exercise for at least two weeks. Without practice, no habit is going to stick. Some may even require a few months' exercise time before you see them take root and make a difference in your life.

This book is divided into three sections.

- The first section, which is foundational to the rest of the book, reveals how our thinking influences our spiritual and emotional health. Its purpose is motivational.

- The second section presents the ten most important habits of the mind. Its purpose is to illustrate how you can change your thinking.

- The third section presents some very specific exercises that can be used by the reader to shape a healthier mind. Its purpose is instructive.

I have a few final words to those of my readers who, like me, are deeply religious. If you are committed in faith to Christ and seek to follow in His steps, what I have to say is particularly important for you. Being a Christian does not in and of itself guarantee that you are healthy in mind and spirit. Our faith provides the resources for healthiness, but chances are you have not been consistent in drawing on these resources for your own healing. You may be in emotional pain, even as you read. You may have faced the most unhappy of life circumstances or have suffered devastating failure.

Well, have hope! You are not entirely to blame for all your failures, and there is something you can do to rise above your unhappy circumstances. I'm not talking about sheer will power, either. The habits I advocate are truly Christ-centered. Take comfort in knowing that you will have His strength to draw on as you seek to change your thinking.

For a theme text I cannot think of a more appropriate verse than Philippians 2:5, "Let this mind be in you, which was also in Christ Jesus." This is my prayer for myself. It is also my prayer for you.

Archibald D. Hart, Ph.D.
Professor of Psychology
Fuller Theological Seminary
Pasadena, California

HABITS OF THE MIND

UNDERSTANDING THE POWER OF THOUGHT

Thoughts are the essential ingredients for living, and they underlie all our actions and feelings. They differentiate us from animals. In this section we will lay a foundation for healthy thinking. I will show how important healthy thinking is and how it influences the body, mind, and spirit.

Thoughts are also the bedrock of our spiritual life and define who we are. Healthy thoughts do not happen by chance but are the product of carefully crafted habits of the mind. If we want to improve our circumstances and emotions, we must first be willing to improve our thoughts. God does not abandon us to our own devices here but offers us a "renewing of the mind" in return for our surrender to Him.

CHAPTER 1

You Are What You Think

Man is obviously made for thinking.
Therein lies all his dignity and his merit;
and his whole duty is to think as he ought.
Blaise Pascal

Healthy thought is a thing of stunning beauty, and those who think healthy thoughts are admirable. But a healthy mind does not exist by accident, nor is it passed on to us through our genes. Healthy thinking involves habits of choice. And each of us has to discover these habits for ourselves, generation after generation.

Why are healthy mental habits important? Because they help to direct our lives. Horace Bushnell says it well: "Habits are to the soul what the veins and arteries are to the blood." He implies that our lives flow through passageways that are established in our thinking as habits. Without these established ways of thinking, we have no clear pathway to guide us when life becomes chaotic.

Habits of the mind also define who we are. Charles Reade picks up on this idea in his much-quoted maxim:

Sow an act and you reap a habit.
Sow a habit and you reap a character.
Sow a character and you reap a destiny.

Habits of the mind ultimately determine our destiny—not only our spiritual destiny but also for our success or failure as individuals. If you study successful people, you will usually discover men and women who have a healthy way of thinking. Even failures don't devastate these individuals because they know how to deal with them.

Furthermore, if you want to know whether or not you are a "good" person, you need look no further than your thinking. Thoughts define character. For example, a dirty mind bespeaks a murky character; a deceitful mind indicates an untrustworthy character. You can't hide from your thought process—it goes with you everywhere, because it is the essence of who you are.

Bad Habits Dominate the Modern Mind

Unfortunately, bad habits are much easier to pick up than good ones, as any parent of a five-year-old will tell you. Nowhere is this truer than in the realm of the mind. This is why we have so many emotionally troubled people in today's world. The modern mind is corrupt, not only because it is sinful, but because it is dominated by unhealthy habits.

In many respects we are better informed than our forebears were, yet we don't seem to be more stable. I know I am more intellectually developed than my grandfather was, although he was someone I loved and respected very much. But I think he had healthier mental habits. And a healthy mind has more to do with habits than with intelligence.

From time to time, we all indulge in the greatest activity of the human mind—thinking. Some of us indulge in it for hours on end and are aware of every passing idea. Others would be hard pressed to recall any time given to thinking. Their thoughts seem to pass through their minds like silent ships in the night. Nevertheless, human beings do think. Although we may not be aware of it, we constantly reason and reflect.

How important is your thought life? Does it really matter what flows through your stream of consciousness? Do you really have to avoid polluting the river of thought in order to preserve your mind's environment? Even more importantly, to what extent does one's mental activity indicate the quality of person one is? Does it reflect the influence of Jesus Christ?

Let me put the issue to you in a nutshell: Who you are, as a Christian believer, can be no better and no worse than the thoughts you entertain in your head. Who you are emotionally can never transcend your level of thinking. Your thought process is a ceiling beyond which you cannot aspire. Your brain is no stronger than your weakest thought, and your character no more virtuous than your most private reflections.

The Influence of Thought

Research has shown that one's thought life influences every aspect of one's being. Figure 1 summarizes some of the more important influences.

THE INFLUENCES OF THOUGHT

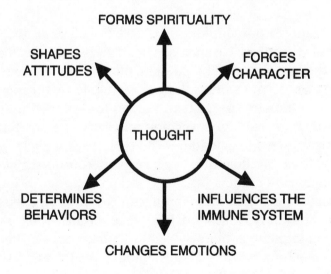

FORMS SPIRITUALITY

SHAPES
ATTITUDES

FORGES
CHARACTER

THOUGHT

DETERMINES
BEHAVIORS

INFLUENCES THE
IMMUNE SYSTEM

CHANGES EMOTIONS

FIGURE 1

Everything about us is constantly being shaped by the stream of our ideas. These ideas take the form of recalled memories, self-conversation, and reflection. They comprise the thoughts that flow through our conscious and not-so-conscious minds.

Your thinking determines whether you move toward disease or health, success or failure, achievement or decline. It influences whether you will live a long or short life and whether you will be happy or sad most of the time. It even determines if you'll get married and whether your sex life will be satisfying.

At the turn of this century, James Allen, an English clergyman, wrote a remarkable little devotional called *As a Man Thinketh*, based on Proverbs 23:7a, which says, "For as he thinketh in his heart, so is he." For nine decades this book has inspired countless numbers of people through its central message: Good thoughts can never produce bad results; bad thoughts can never produce good results. This formula is so simple that we ought to teach it vigorously in our schools and preach it more passionately from our pulpits.

Don't Underestimate the Power of Thought

Our capacity for thinking is foundational to all the brain's marvelous functions. No matter what action you take, it is both anticipated and followed by thought. But thought can exist without action, too. For example, I don't have to leave the comfort of my favorite lounge chair to take a grand tour of the Rhine River. I can settle back, close my eyes, and relive my last trip down that mighty river in my imagination. I can recapture the sights, sounds, and smells of the beautiful vine-covered countryside and the majestic, ancient castles.

If I am feeling blue, I can indulge in reliving some wonderful moments from my childhood. I can take a walk in my imagination down to the river below my grandfather's house. There I can spend a few hours fishing and listening to his tales of adventure during the Anglo-Boer War, during a time when wild lions roamed freely across South Africa.

Imagination is powerful, but thought goes beyond imagination in its power. Whether we examine mental health, physical disease, success, or happiness modern psychology is discovering something that the Bible has told us for centuries: You are the product of your thoughts. The mind determines who and what we are as individuals.

A kind person thinks kind thoughts. A contented person thinks contented thoughts. The same can be said about people who are successful or are enjoying a well-deserved retirement. They live out what they think. The mind is healthy, so the living is healthy. John Chapman wrote,

> Our goodness comes solely from thinking on goodness; our wickedness from thinking on wickedness.

The theme of this book is quite simple. If you want to be happy and successful, you must learn how to be a healthy thinker. Every effective person has a wholesome pattern of thinking. Every troubled person has a troubled mind. When thoughts are crazy, life is crazy. Bad thinking can destroy our lives just as cancer can destroy our bodies.

How does thinking affect one's spiritual life? Scripture is full of references to this process. Perhaps the best known is Philippians 4:8, where Paul writes,

> And now, brothers, as I close this letter let me say this one more thing: Fix your thoughts on what is true and good and right. Think about things that are pure and lovely, and dwell on the fine good things in others. Think about all you can praise God for and be glad about. Keep putting into practice all you learned from me and saw me doing, and the God of peace will be with you. (TLB)

That just about says it all, doesn't it?

The Elements of Healthy Thinking

How do we comply with these commands? Throughout the chapters that follow, I will focus on two key principles:

First, healthy thinking is a habit we have to learn. We are not born with it; in fact much of our early life seems to have worked against us by establishing unhealthy habits of thinking. We may well have to unlearn some bad habits before we can begin to learn healthier ones.

Second, thought always comes before feeling and action. In other words, if you want to influence how you feel or how you behave, you must first pay attention to how you think. The attention must be intentional and specific. Many unhappy people complain about their miserable feelings without realizing that they can change those feelings through healthier thinking.

That second point deserves some elaboration. It amazes me how often I encounter patients who, despite much personal pain and many repetitive mistakes, never grasp this fundamental fact: You cannot control your feelings directly, only indirectly through your thoughts. If we conscientiously put this principle into practice we would save ourselves a fortune wasted on ineffective psychotherapy.

I speak as a psychotherapist. And my estimate is that about 75 percent of the psychotherapy delivered across the country is of little value precisely because it focuses too much on past hurts, unmerited self-aggrandizement, and a culture of anger enhancement. It would be a lot more effective if it focused on the present and what a troubled person can do to change unhappy circumstances. In short, *Change your thoughts first, and the desired feelings will follow.*

What about Feelings?

Unfortunately, many people tend to react to life more emotionally than mentally. They mess up their lives by allowing themselves to be driven by apparently uncontrollable emotions, feelings they seem helpless to resist. One hears it all the time in therapy: "My father doesn't respect me for what I do, so I become depressed. I can't help it!" Or, "My wife isn't interested in sex, and I just don't seem able to shake myself out of a sulk when she denies me."

The theme is always present: "I can't help my feelings." People believe that emotions are beyond our reach or influence and that we must passively allow feelings to work out their devastation without any resistance whatsoever. If there is one big lie our therapeutic age has fostered, it is the lie that feelings are all-powerful and cannot be challenged. I suppose it's good for business.

It is true that we cannot overcome certain feelings by tackling them head-on and trying to defeat them with sheer will power. We have to tackle them indirectly, through influencing the thoughts that cause them. Feelings are the consequence, not the cause, of our emotional problems. This truth opens up a whole new world of freedom and control for all of us.

Now don't misunderstand me. Feelings are important—very important. They are key sources of information about what is going on inside us. Our feelings can originate in deeply unconscious fears—fears we cannot rationally explain or even bring into our awareness. Some of these fears are deeply conditioned into us, and no amount of thinking is going to explain or remove them. Ask any sufferer of a severe phobia about this. Logic doesn't cure the phobia by itself. It needs a little help from other sources as well.

Feelings are signals, warning signs, like emotional flashing red lights or smoke alarms. They warn us about violations to our well-being, or they indicate impending danger. They alert us to the deeper mental processes that disturb our tranquility or distort our perceptions. Feelings like this must be attended to and explored, even in psychotherapy if necessary, to get at the source of this danger and to find some understanding of what is wrong.

But feelings can also be unreliable and unpredictable. You cannot always trust them, just as you cannot always trust a smoke alarm. The one in my kitchen gives more false alarms than real ones. It has sent me many sinister messages in the dead of night without any threat of fire. But I've not thrown it out, because someday it may serve a useful purpose. In the meantime, it is up to me to determine whether its warnings are true or false.

Likewise, when we respond to life's challenges, we must first respond with our heads (thinking), then with our hearts (feeling). Whatever we do, we must never use our hearts without our heads. A heart without a head is like a boat without a rudder or a train without a track.

Sometimes, and I must emphasize *sometimes*, your heart may be more right than your head. As Jacques Boussuel has said, "The heart has reasons that reason does not understand." But more often than not, the heart tends to get in the way of sensibility. I can't begin to tell you how often I've come across people who have trusted their hearts over their heads and have lived to regret it. Eventually they've come to their senses—but it was too late.

The area of life where this mistake is made most is, as you would suspect, in the area of romance. In this realm the heart always asserts itself and tries to dominate the head. This is so much the case that romance easily blinds us to certain realities that, if we could only keep our sanity, our head would see quite readily. The problem is that romantic love is really a temporary form of insanity (my tongue is halfway in my cheek, of course) that blinds our rational eyes. Unfortunately, the cure for this blindness may only come when romance has faded and one realizes that feelings can't always be trusted by themselves. There must be a sensible counterbalance: Never use your heart without your head.

But this raises a very important question: what if my head is not trustworthy? That is what this book is all about. I will try to provide practical advice on how we can teach our heads to be healthier, our minds to be saner, and thus our feelings to be more reliable. I will use many biblical truths to make my points, simply because I believe God knows us intimately, and He is well aware of the guidance we need to function in wholeness and health.

Beware Too Much Logic

While this book will emphasize the importance of being logical and rational, I want to avoid the mistake of advocating extreme rationality. Too much logic can be a handicap, and I say this as a person who tries to be exceptionally logical.

I knew someone once who prided himself in being super logical. He had explanations for everything. What amazed me was how often he was wrong. He could only see extremes, never shades of gray. And the gray areas of life are simply not amenable to logic. We cannot explain everything, just as we cannot understand everything. We cannot reason our way out of every problem. We cannot answer every question. We can't even ask the right questions most of the time. Some things are best accepted simply for what they are.

Ruthless logic is a sign of a limited mind. It must have strict rules because it cannot think for itself. Somewhere, we must make room for faith and hope, and they are not always strictly rational or logical.

A healthy mind has the freedom to escape its natural gravity and soar into space, to escape the mundane, to be creative and to see things from different perspectives. It has the ability, sometimes, to defy logic and cold reason, and to take risks, even when common sense says it shouldn't. Or, braver still, it may decide to do the opposite of what friends have warned against. Such freedom to be novel and creative is the seed from which greatness of spirit grows. No one has ever achieved real greatness without the ability to occasionally fly in the face of frigid logic and reason.

Having said all that, good and healthy thinking has the power to change your life. Without a healthy mind you cannot be a healthy person. As Thomas L. Masson says, "No brain is stronger than its weakest think." Healthy thinking takes us out of emotional slavery into freedom and promise. Most people, as William James notes, live in a very restricted circle of their potential being. This is the case because they only use a small portion of their conscious minds.

Thinking affects every aspect of our being. Emotional and mental health, personal happiness, work efficiency and satisfaction, level of success, as well as physical health and a healthy immune system are all related to and dependent upon having a healthy mind. James Allen puts it as clearly as anyone: "The body is the servant of the mind. It obeys the operations of the mind, whether they be deliberately chosen or automatically expressed. . . . Disease and health, like circumstances, are rooted in thought."

An Important Difference

What I am advocating here should in no way be likened to belief systems such as Christian Science. In fact, what Christian

Science advocates is about as far away from reality and biblical principles as you can get. It is a system that fosters an enormous denial of reality. Also, all concepts of "mind over matter" are clearly unacceptable. The mind cannot control matter. I wish it could—it would make it all so simple. But the mind cannot bend spoons or see through walls. Such phenomena have clearly been debunked as trickery and wishful thinking.

As we proceed I will be very careful to avoid ideas that are questionable and untruthful. In fact, I will not use any ideas similar to those of Christian Science because I do not believe they are valid. Rather, I will show how a truly biblical model differs from these distortions. Our task is not only to learn healthier ways of thinking. It is also to break some of the bad habits of thought we have established over many years. With God's help, I believe we can do both.

CHAPTER 2

THE POWER OF ONE THOUGHT

All that a man achieves
and all that he fails to achieve
is the direct result of his own thoughts.
James Allen

Before we can even begin to contemplate a healthy mind, we need to consider the basic building blocks of the mind—our thoughts. Thoughts are the essential components of our physical life. The ability to think makes it possible for us to be human.

Thought is also the essence of our spiritual life. Just to be able to fathom what God has done for us in Christ takes understanding, and understanding is a form of thought. To recognize our sin, to reach out for forgiveness, to take up our cross and follow our Master involves the most profound of thoughts. To be inspired by Scripture, to come to terms with our need to receive and give love, to delight in the radiance of God's presence in some moment of prayerful communion requires thinking. We cannot avoid thought and still become vibrant, vital spiritual or psychological beings. And that brings us to the intriguing topic of this chapter: How powerful is a thought?

In physical terms a thought consumes the power of a few micro-milliwatts of energy. This amounts to just one or two thousandths of a millionth of a watt. How little is this? The clearest way I can describe it is to say that it would take sixty billion simultaneous thoughts to light an ordinary reading light bulb. And you would have to think all these thoughts at one time and keep going to keep this page lit.

Clearly, there's not a lot of physical energy flowing through your brain when you think. But what a lot of "other" power there is in one thought—power that makes each thought a miracle of creation! A short burst of thoughts, be it ever so humble, is able to change the world. Human history is full of examples.

The Achievements of Great Thought

Everything ever achieved, whether bad or good, began as thought. Adolf Hitler thought about creating a master race before he nearly destroyed a civilization. Jim Jones thought he was a god and led nine hundred or more of his followers to their destruction. Albert Einstein contemplated a few carefully orchestrated thoughts and set the stage for the use of atomic energy. Beethoven thought a few musical thoughts and gave us the Fifth Symphony. Winston Churchill could articulate his thoughts like no one else in his day and mobilized morale to save England from Nazi domination.

The Magna Carta, the Eiffel Tower, the Mona Lisa, the Declaration of Independence, the Sistine Chapel, the Pyramids of Egypt, and the Great Wall of China—all these began as thought in someone's mind. Even my very existence on God's earth, and yours, began as a thought.

Of course it is not thought that works the wonders. If an idea never gets beyond flitting about in someone's head it can accomplish nothing. It is when thoughts influence behavior and motivate the human mind to action that power is released. Thoughts have influence because they control the center of power and possess the ability to initiate or stifle activity. Without thought there can be no purposeful human action, because action without meaningful thought is just crazy behavior.

Thoughts Are at the Center of Existence

To understand how something as minuscule as a thought can become a symphony or an atomic bomb, we have to understand that thoughts are the center of our existence. They have a dramatic effect on our mind, body, and emotions, and their effect is automatic. Strange as it seems, we don't have to think about thinking—we're already doing it.

Every waking moment of every day we choose and encourage thoughts, and those thoughts shape our character and form our destiny. And the way we hang on to some thoughts, choosing them over others, amounts to a set of habits we form over the years—the habits of the mind.

The best analogy I can provide is that of a horse. Imagine a racehorse, powerful, full of energy, and high-spirited. If I scare it, it will bolt. How do I harness the horse's power? With a bridle. The horse learns the "habit signals" of the bridle and obeys its every movement. Turn left. Turn right. Gallop. Stop. The power is not in the bridle, but in the horse's muscles and adrenaline. But the control exerted by the bridle imposes power over the horse.

So also are habits of the mind. They are the controls, the signals that start and stop certain activities. We are not slaves to our minds, but we are slaves to the habits that control our minds. We weave patterns of thought out of ignorance and neglect. We let bad habits become dominant.

The result? Pain and unhappiness, self-defeat and self-destruction. James Allen is right when he says that our mind is the "master weaver, forming both the inner garment of our character and the outer garment of circumstances."[1] The mind defines who we are and creates our environment. Our ugliness or beauty is both on the inside and the outside, shaped by the same forces.

Our mind, not our feelings or actions, ultimately shapes our destiny because it is the bridle that holds the power of control. We are what we think, and how we think is controlled by the habits of the mind ingrained in us from our earliest years, as much a part of our personality as our feelings, actions, and reactions. Changing our way of thinking often transforms some aspects of our personality.

The Power of Thought

Much has been written about the power of thought. Some of it is grossly simplified and exaggerated and neglects other important aspects of our being. For instance, can I really achieve anything I want by sheer thinking? There are those who say that you can accomplish anything you want just by imagining it. Suppose you want to be a great composer. You just visualize yourself in that role, and you will bring it about quite magically. Those who teach such things say, "Think it and it is yours."

Books on the subject abound. *Success through Positive Mental Attitude. Success Unlimited.* Success always figures in the title or subtitle of these books. You can accomplish anything you wish, provided you want it strongly enough.

Is all this true? I doubt it. There is no free lunch when it comes to being successful. Success takes a lot of hard work, along with the good fortune of being at the right place at the right time. In actual fact, we walk a narrow road between overemphasizing thought to the neglect of action or overemphasizing action to the neglect of thought. Some people have the right thoughts but insufficient action. Others are ready to spring into action but lack the right thoughts. Success eludes both.

The Power of ONE Thought

It doesn't take a lot of thought to determine the difference between success and failure. It only takes one thought. Again and again you will notice that I am emphasizing the power of one tiny, apparently insignificant thought. This thought can make the difference between health and sickness, happiness and misery, victory and defeat. A healthy mind watches the little thoughts that take root in the unattended crevices of the mind-soil. If they are good thoughts, they should be watered and tended. If they are bad thoughts they should be quickly eradicated.

Remember the adage of Benjamin Franklin:

> For want of a nail the shoe was lost; for want of a shoe the horse was lost; for want of a horse the rider was lost and for want of a rider the battle was lost.

It is the "nail" of little thoughts with which we should be concerned. The power of one insignificant thought was illuminated for me a few years ago when I first read Bryce Courteney's beautiful novel about my South African homeland entitled *The Power of One*. The book profoundly impacted me because it describes an era in the history of South Africa that virtually paralleled my own life. The places described, the racial tensions, and the formidable situations that the young hero had to survive were as familiar to me as they were to the novelist.

Nicknamed "PK," the young hero of the novel is sent to a boarding school at a very young age because of his mother's nervous breakdown. He is then raised in the rural countryside by an aunt. In the style of Dickens, the author describes one unhappy experience after another in this young boy's life. Yet frightful as they were, or perhaps because of them, the young boy survives those experiences to become a person of outstanding character.

One day, while making a long train journey home to his mother, PK becomes acquainted with the train conductor, Hoppie Groenewald. Hoppie is a former boxer, and in his countrified, uneducated wisdom, he teaches the boy how to survive in a tough world by understanding the power that one thought or action can have in his life. From this principle is drawn the title of the novel, *The Power of One*.

Only briefly did Hoppie pass through the young boy's life, in fact he knows him for only twenty-four hours. Yet Hoppie teaches PK that there is immense power in one thought, one idea, one heart, one mind, one plan, one determination. This belief gives PK hope at a time when he thought the world around him had been specially arranged to bring about his undoing. At last PK has a defense against future disappointments. The power of one was to be a flame in the little boy's heart that would never be extinguished. He knew that as long as it burned within him, he could never be destroyed.

Don't Neglect Your Little Thoughts

A potent example of the importance of little things, such as the thoughts we allow to hang about in our heads, is described by Og Mandino in his little book, *A Better Way to Live*. He suggests that if you are ever in New York with a few hours to spare that you take a helicopter ride over the top of the Statue of Liberty. As you approach the Lady, standing 305 feet above sea level, and look down at the top of her head, you will note that every strand of her hair has been painstakingly formed in careful and minute detail, like every other part of her. Yet the top of her head is hidden from view.

What is so unusual about this? The delicate coiffure at the top of Liberty's head required many additional weeks of toil in the workshop of the master sculptor. Those weeks of work could have been saved by a less detailed representation of the hair on the top of her head—especially since, in the 1880s, there was no way of looking at the top of her head. There were no airplanes and no helicopters—only the sea gulls would see.

But the master sculptor, Auguste Bartholdi, took no shortcuts. Even though he believed it would never catch anyone's eye, he shaped every strand of her head, seen or unseen, as if all of it would be scrutinized from close quarters. He was a true craftsman.

I suggest that we do the same with every idea in our heads. Each residing thought or belief needs to be given the utmost care in its formation, whether or not it will be evident to others. Sooner or later, a thought stuck away in the dark recesses of our mind will begin to exert its influence.

A Place for "Reality Thinking"

Of course, the counterbalance is this: While thoughts are powerful, more powerful than most people realize, they are not all-powerful. Thoughts are not reality. Thoughts cannot cause food to materialize, nor can they save abused children, no matter how positive they are. You can think positive thoughts until your head has enlarged a few hat sizes, but your most positive thoughts cannot find you a job unless you apply for one. Thoughts cannot cure your appendicitis unless you visit your surgeon.

I sometimes think that positive thinking has become a holier-than-thou form of denial in our Christian subculture. For many, a certain style of refusal to accept reality has become equivalent to "faith." When faced with a serious tragedy or hopeless life circumstance, you are told to have faith, meaning that you should ignore the reality of your circumstance and go forward as if it didn't exist. It has become a justification for not being able to accept the moment for what it is—good or bad.

Now don't misunderstand me. Negative thinking is not the alternative. What sort of thinking is the healthiest? If I were to give it a name it would be "Reality Thinking," which I will be discussing it later in this book. God doesn't call us to look at everything as if it were perfect, without flaws. Sometimes the glass is half empty, not half full. Sometimes what we are experiencing is horrible and has no redeeming features.

When we see the faces of starving children or the bodies of thousands of people who have been massacred somewhere in the world, how can we just think positively? Only realistic thoughts in response to real problems will ever change abominable circumstances into tolerable ones.

So is negative thinking ever realistic? No, it is not. Negative thinking is always a distortion and never constructive. Reality thinking can be positive in its effects, but it avoids any form of positive reasoning that is a disguise for denial.

A Deep Personal Loss

The inadequacy of positive thinking becomes all too clear when one is faced with loss. I mean real loss. Only a few weeks before writing this chapter, our family experienced a most horrible tragedy. My wife and I had been out to dinner with some friends and arrived home at about 9 P.M. Shortly afterward the telephone rang. It was Sharon, my middle daughter, and she was troubled. Her husband Richard hadn't come home from work as expected.

Richard was a schoolteacher who also coached swimming, and he was usually home by 8 P.M. Sharon was particularly worried because the school had called to say that he had never arrived there. She had telephoned around but had been unable to locate him. Then she called the county hospital trauma center and was told that they had a John Doe who had been critically injured. Would she come immediately in case it was Richard? Sharon asked if I would take her to the hospital, some ten miles away.

Driving to the trauma center was a nightmare. We didn't know what was waiting for us. What could I say to my daughter? Think positively? It wouldn't change a thing. Judging by the description the hospital had given Sharon, the chances were very strong that we would find Richard there. Nearly ten hours before, a patient had been airlifted to the hospital by helicopter following a freeway accident. His identification was not on him. Sharon knew that Richard kept his wallet in his briefcase in the trunk of the car.

"Yes," she murmured to me as we drove, "it probably is Richard."

I gave Sharon a gentle nudge toward reality. "Whatever awaits us at the hospital, my darling, we must be willing to accept it from the hand of God. He hasn't caused the accident, but He knows we are hurting. And He will give us whatever strength we need to see us through."

A large trauma center in downtown Los Angeles is not a pretty picture. Shooting victims, derelicts, and the most serious of injuries are sent there because the facility is equipped to handle any trauma. White–coated young doctors took us into a side–room and frankly informed us, "The situation is grave. The patient we have has a 99 percent chance of dying in the next few hours. Be prepared to see a very broken body."

As my daughter responded, I realized that she was the bravest person I had ever seen. "If it's my husband, I want to see him now. Please take me to him."

Together we braced ourselves and walked into the center of the trauma unit, past other patients, tubes, and paraphernalia I can't even describe. We could not tell from the patient's face if it was Richard. But when we pulled back the sheet to look at his body, telltale birthmarks on his legs told us all we needed to know.

Yes, it was Richard. He had swerved to miss a crate that had dropped off a truck on the freeway not far from where he lived. For twelve hours he had been in a coma, with Sharon knowing nothing about it. And now he was critical.

Positive thinking wouldn't change a thing.

Reality stared us in the face.

Richard died three hours later, and we are all still in mourning as I write. My daughter was widowed at thirty-four. Her two sons, aged twelve and nine, have been left without a father. As we face and plan for the future, we do so with all the strength we can muster, relying on the One of all comfort.

I am sure you've faced your share of tragedy as well. And as you know, experiences like this have to be borne with courage. You don't learn much from them in the process; you simply try to endure them with fortitude. You quickly discover how painful life can be, and if you're not careful you can become a resentful cynic about everything. You are not made into some hero by your suffering. You simply accept that this is life, sometimes tragic, always fragile, temporary, and risky.

Healthy Thinking and Faith

Healthy thinking, especially when coupled with a deep trust in the comfort God provides, can see us through life's most painful experiences. It doesn't take us out of them but simply carries us through them. Sometimes organized religion, even Christianity, can work against healthy thinking. It fosters a denial of reality that doesn't draw us closer to God but instead drives a wedge between Him and us. When the chips are down and tragedy befalls us we don't ask, "How can I draw on God's help for me in this situation?" Rather, we ask, "Where is God when I need Him?" God is hard to find when you've allowed faulty thinking to disable your faith.

What is the ultimate goal of a healthy mind? It is not just to be successful. Nor is it to be happy, at least not in a glib or superficial sense. I would say it is to be at peace with yourself and your Creator and to have that calmness of mind that can best be labeled "serenity." James Allen says that calmness of mind is the result of long and patient efforts in self-control, especially control of the laws and operations of thinking.[2] People become serene in the measure that they understand themselves as thought-producing beings. When they can control their own thoughts, they can understand how thoughts motivate others.

When you consider how many people (to quote Allen) "sour their lives and ruin all that is sweet and beautiful by explosive tempers or who destroy their poise of character" by uncontrolled thought, it is clear that we need to recover a greater appreciation for self-control, an appreciation that has slipped from us in modern times. We need to place our hand "firmly upon the helm of thought" and thus take command of our whole lives. Only then will serenity be our experience. Only then can the power of Christ-directed thought be realized, a power that must never be underestimated.

CHAPTER 3

THOUGHTS FORGE YOUR CHARACTER

You are today where your thoughts have brought you;
you will be tomorrow where your thoughts take you.
James Allen

It is hard to fight an enemy who has outposts in your head.
Sally Kempton

The impact of your thought life goes well beyond the creation of serenity and happiness or the removal of vexation. It creates a foundation deep within your soul upon which your very character is built. Your whole being is shaped by what resides in your head. Do you think a great deal about your character? Do you wonder whether you can do anything to improve it?

Some people I know don't seem at all concerned about who they are. All they want is space and freedom to do their thing. They care little about their reputation, or worse yet, they don't seem to care whether or not they have any reputation to defend. Of course, they are often lamentably miserable and see no connection between their unhappiness and their self-centered character. People like this usually blame others for their unhappiness.

In the latter years of my life I have more frequently begun to reflect on my character. And interestingly, this process has come about at a time when I am becoming less concerned about "what other people think." These days, I am more conscious about who I am as a person for my own sake. For me, character has become a personal integrity concern, not a showcase issue. I've been asking myself questions like:

- Am I the person others believe me to be?

- Whether others observe my behavior or not, am I a person of integrity?

- Am I perceived to be an honest person?

- Am I someone who can be trusted?

These questions cut to the core of my being. And the habits of my thought life are the most important diagnostic mirrors of my character. These habits not only describe who I am, they also serve to shape my essential personhood.

I believe we could all do with some improvement and discipline in our characters. It is very clear that a good character does not come about automatically. It is not a thing of chance any more than a beautiful garden is. It takes conscious effort, deliberate planning and intention, and a lot of gut-wrenching courage to persist in shaping one's character. As James Allen puts it: "A noble and Godlike character is not a thing of favor or chance, but is the natural result of continued effort in right thinking, the effect of long-cherished association with Godlike thoughts."

By the same means, we can form our characters into ignoble and bestial ones. If we harbor dishonorable and degrading thoughts, if we fill our minds with filth and hate, if profanity punctuates our self-talk, we not only fail to establish a good character but deliberately shape a bad one. It is the abuse and wrong application of our thoughts that pulls us down to the level of the beast.

The Beast within Us All

A few days after my son-in-law, Richard, was killed, while clearing out one of his drawers, I discovered that he had purchased two tickets for *Beauty and the Beast* at the Schubert Theater in Los Angeles. They were meant to be a surprise for Sharon's birthday. I showed them to her and asked what she wanted to do with them. Because she wished to honor Richard's idea for celebrating her birthday, Sharon asked me to take her to the show in Richard's place.

Sitting in the Schubert Theater that evening was a very moving experience for both of us, given the special circumstances. It is not surprising that the story and music from *Beauty and the Beast* has become very special to me.

The story is about a disgusting beggar woman who offers a selfish and unkind prince a beautiful rose in return for shelter in his castle on a bitter cold night. The prince is repulsed by her ugly appearance and turns her away. She warns him not to be deceived by appearances, but he will have none of her advice.

In fact, it turns out that she is, in reality, a beautiful enchantress, and she turns the prince into an ugly beast because of his unkindness. To become normal again, she explains that the prince has to learn how to love another person and to get someone to return his love before the enchanted rose drops its last petal.

Ashamed of his appearance, the prince, who is now an ugly beast, fears that no one can love him as he is, so he becomes a recluse, hiding from the world. The years roll by. One petal after another falls to the ground. Finally the heroine arrives on the scene, as in all good fairy stories, and slowly begins to change the beast. Whereas he was ugly on both the inside and outside, he now begins to change and becomes beautiful on the inside. They come to love each other, and he returns to being a handsome young prince. Finally, he is beautiful on both the inside and outside.

What struck me about the story is that we all have something of the beast inside us. Sin sees to that. We are selfish, self-centered, and short on caring for others. Most of us are unmindful of this, far more concerned about what we are on the outside than what we are on the inside. And until we can get someone to love us for who we really are, we will remain ugly on the inside.

Thank God who sent Christ to demonstrate that very kind of love. Because He loved us in spite of all our sinful ugliness, we have the potential to become beautiful on the inside. I came away from *Beauty and the Beast* with a greater determination to pay attention to the ugliness inside me. That is, after all, what sanctification is all about.

How Do We Gauge Character?

What is the touchstone of your character? How can you measure it, and against what standard do you compare it? The other day, I was showing one of my granddaughters how we can determine whether a ring is made of genuine gold or of some artificial metal. She had been given a ring as a present and was wondering if it was real or fake. I pulled out a small, gray piece of polished stone from my jewelry-making drawer and rubbed the ring across it. It was fake.

"What is that?" She looked at the stone curiously.

"It is called a touchstone." I explained. "When you rub metal across it the metal leaves a mark. With a little practice you can tell real gold from fake by the color of the mark."

I was born in the diamond mining area of South Africa and grew up in the gold mining area. A fascination with diamonds and gold is in my veins, and one of the many hobbies I have developed over the years is goldsmithing. I've always owned a touchstone, ever since I can remember. A touchstone is a type of dense, siliceous stone used since ancient times to test the purity of gold and silver.

Character has its touchstone too. It is our thought life. Our character is continuously being streaked by our thoughts. These thoughts reveal to God and to ourselves what sort of persons we really are.

Character is difficult to gauge, because so much of it involves the secret, hidden things of life. It's a lot easier to talk about intelligence because we can see it, and it is measurable. So are traits such as bad temper or pervasive prejudices. Our actions shout out loud and clear, telling the world how many negative traits we have.

But character is much broader than these traits. It permeates deeper and involves far more of our soul. It operates behind the scenes, influencing our desires, motives, actions, and reactions. In the final analysis, character makes or unmakes us.

Leon Trotsky, the Russian revolutionary of the early part of this century, believed that character is most often revealed when we are removed from the safe conditions of life, for only then are we thrown back to the reserves of our inner selves. This implies that character is more than a present trait. It is a reservoir of resources that we can fall back on, a foundation of goodness that elevates us in times of crisis, a set of attitudes that determines how we respond to life's challenges.

A Man of Highest Character

One of the most moving stories about the deeper influences of character on the shape of a person's life goes back to the fifteenth century. As told by Og Mandino, there lived in a tiny village near Nuremberg, Germany, a man by the name of Albrecht Durer. He worked as a goldsmith to support his wife and eighteen children. Because times were hard, he also did other chores around the village to help relieve his family's pitiful condition.

Despite their plight, two of Durer's children, Albrecht and Albert, had a dream. They had worked with their father, learning the skills of the goldsmith in his workshop, and they showed much promise. They both wanted to become great artists. They knew their father couldn't afford to send one of them to the academy in Nuremberg to study, let alone both of them, so after long discussions at night in their crowded home, the brothers devised a plan. They would select one brother by chance who would go to work in the nearby mines. With his earnings he would support the other brother at the academy. After four years, they would reverse their roles.

They tossed a coin and Albrecht Durer won. Albert, the loser, set off for the mines.

For the next four years Albrecht studied hard. Woodcuts, oils, etchings, watercolors—there was no art form he did not master. At every point of art he was better than his professors. He thrived and it began to look as if he might become famous and wealthy one day.

In the meantime, Albert continued his perilous work in the mines, waiting for the day his turn would come to enter the art world.

Finally the brothers returned to a festive, triumphant dinner celebration. Near the end of the meal, Albrecht raised a toast to his brother, who had sacrificed four years of his life to give him a headstart toward his ambition. "Now Albert, blessed brother of mine, now it is your turn! I will take care of you while you go and study."

All heads turned to Albert. But he sat sobbing in his chair, repeating again and again, "No . . . no . . . no . . ."

At last he arose, raised his hands to his face so all could see them and began to speak. "See what four years in the mines have done!" Everyone gasped as he displayed his disfigured hands. Every finger had been broken or crushed at least once. The scars of his toil and sacrifice were patently obvious. "For me," he quietly concluded, "it is too late."

Albert would never be able to draw or paint. Delicate lines of pen or paint would no longer be possible. He had given the ultimate sacrifice for his brother—his hands.

The story doesn't end there. No doubt you have seen the homage that Albrecht Durer paid his brother in later life. It is the painstakingly accurate portrait of his brother's hands, painted with love and gratitude. Albrecht simply titled the painting "Hands." The world, however, moved by the masterpiece, renamed it "The Praying Hands." Today art lovers admire this great memorial to personal reverence, but most don't comprehend its real significance.

What made it possible for Albert to work those long years for his brother's sake? What helped him bear the horror of crushed fingers at a time when there was no medical science to speak of, and no painkillers to relieve his suffering? What kept him from resentment, envy, and jealousy? I can think of only one answer: Albert Durer was a man of monumental character.

God Calls Us to Build Our Character

The Bible makes no direct references to the concept of character. Instead, the term "walk" is used to express this idea. Our "walk" describes the way we conduct the aspects of life that define our character. Isaiah says, "They that wait upon the LORD . . . shall walk, and not faint" (40:31). This is not a reference to physical walking but rather to the way we conduct our lives.

Paul instructs us to "Walk by faith" (2 Cor. 5:7), and "Walk in the Spirit" (Gal. 5:16).

Finally, we are told to "Walk, even as he walked" (1 John 2:6). Walking, in all these references, refers to the totality of our living. The way we walk is a direct expression of our character.

Most of us are able to recognize people we know from a distance by observing the way they walk. Their ambling, strolling, or sauntering is every bit as characteristic as their fingerprints. The same is true of character. It identifies us as incontestably as our physical walk.

One of the clearest truths that Scripture teaches us is that we don't have to accept our character as it is; we can be transformed. Furthermore, we can imprint the character of Christ upon our own inner selves. The clearest reference to this is found in Romans 12:2: "And be not conformed to this world: but be ye transformed by the renewing of your mind, that ye may prove what is that good, and acceptable, and perfect, will of God."

I love this verse because it holds out so much hope for recovery from whatever damage our characters may have suffered due to bad genes or unfavorable circumstances. We are not imprisoned by our histories. There is a way out of all past damage.

However, there is one catch. It is Christ's character that is imprinted on you as you walk the Christ-road. And some people are not all that enamored with holiness, righteousness, grace, goodness, sacrifice, and the other characteristics of the Christ-life. But what alternative character is there? Where is there a more beautiful expression of humanness? What equivalent goodness is to be found in anyone else—politicians, philosophers, or worse yet, psychologists? To what and to whom do we turn for a model of good character if we turn our backs on Christ?

As you continue to read, you will see that I firmly believe our minds are healthier when we are developing Christlike character. Living a lie cannot produce a good life, but truth will never let us down. How can we tell the truth about life from its many lies? By paying attention to our thoughts and the way we think our thoughts. By becoming intimate with the One who can help us think pure and healthy thoughts. By letting God sanctify our minds.

In the final analysis, the key to wholesome and healthy living lies in being attached to the Source of all wholeness, our Lord Himself. Besides suggesting ways you can open yourself, and especially your mind, to greater health and effectiveness, I also suggest that you be open to the nature of Christ. Without Him, your strength of character will be superficial and will snap when stretched by the real strains and struggles of life. With Him, strength of character will be the natural by–product of a transformed mind.

CHAPTER 4

SHAPING HEALTHY MENTAL HABITS

A man's mind may be likened to a garden,
which may be intelligently cultivated
or allowed to run wild; but whether cultivated
or neglected, it must, and will, bring forth.
James Allen

The habits that make up a healthy mind have not changed appreciably for thousands of years. Ancient writings reveal that the qualities constituting a healthy mind are universal and timeless, and examples abound in the writings of the great philosophers. But besides philosophers, other thinking persons also show evidence of this. Marcus Aurelius was born in A.D. 121 and became emperor of Rome at age forty. He was a just and merciful ruler, and during his campaigns he wrote Meditations in which he emphasized the value of right thought. His most famous statement is:

> If thou art pained by an external thing, it is not this thing
> that disturbs thee, but thy own judgment (or thought) about it.
> And it is in thy power to wipe out this judgment now.[1]

It is a mistake to think that psychology is relatively new or that we have only recently invented ways to understand the mind. The formal science of psychology may be of recent origin, but scholars have observed the functioning of the mind for many centuries. Although we possess more information about the mind than our grandparents, people have been observing people ever since the dawn of time. It is very clear that the ancients knew much about the mind and its activities. They knew that bad mental states caused illness, that a healthy mind could create a state of happiness, and that it was important to observe and change unwholesome thoughts.

Is Psychology in the Bible?

An important question for many believers is how psychology fits into Scripture. As a Christian psychologist I have spent a large part of my life integrating my faith with my psychology. My conclusion is this: The most profound psychology is found, quite appropriately, in our own Bible. There are many references to *thought* and the *mind*.

Much of our contemporary Christian resistance to anything psychological stems from our reaction to statements Sigmund Freud made early in this century. Most notably, he labeled those of us who were religious as "neurotic." We therefore turned our backs on Freud and have remained suspicious ever since. I'm not surprised by this. Much that he said was problematic. But we are never wise to throw the baby out with the bathwater.

One of the ways we can restore a balanced view of psychology is to read the works of outstanding Christian leaders who wrote before Freud. Oswald Chambers is a good example. He was the author of *My Utmost for His Highest*, perhaps the world's most celebrated collection of daily devotional readings. But Chambers also wrote a rather remarkable book at the turn of the century entitled *Biblical Psychology*. Used as a textbook at the Bible Training College, London, in 1917, it is a much neglected resource, probably due to our high-tech fixation with everything modern.

This fascinating text clearly demonstrates just how psychologically relevant the teachings of Scripture are to our thoughts and minds. It is also free of the post-Freudian paranoia that characterizes so much contemporary Christian teaching in some quarters. The bottom line of Oswald Chambers' thesis is this:

You cannot remove the mind and its activities from the spirit. They are inseparably bound together—no mind, no person.

The Pace of Modern Life

As Christians in search of healthy minds, our faith—walk with God through Christ has a lot to offer us in terms of greater maturity and a Christlike character. We can draw much from the ageless wisdom of Scripture. But there is a key difference between our modern world and that of past generations. Today's world moves at a pace unheard-of in earlier times, and this pace of modern life is often our undoing. It robs us of the time we need for reflection. More often than I care to remember I have heard a patient say to me: "I haven't had a moment this week to think about what we talked about last week." I believe him or her, yet it seems strange. Where does all the time go?

Without stretching the metaphor much at all, the modern world can be described as moving with lightning speed. In comparison, my grandfather lived an extremely slow-paced life. Even as a young child I found it slow. It was not that he didn't have a lot of energy or vitality. He was one of the most vibrant and creative people I have ever known. Nor was he lazy. However, his life didn't involve a lot of complexity. It was slow because there was only a narrow country lane that ran past the front door of his home, unlike the freeway that runs past mine.

Nowadays it feels as if the world's greatest superhighway runs directly through my brain. In fact, that is close to the truth. The speed of computers, and the capability we now have to instantaneously transfer information around the world has placed many of us in the fast lane of the information super-highway, whether or not we wish to be there.

Hurriedness and the Human Mind

What has this fast pace of our life got to do with the habits of a healthy mind? Many things, but here I want to particularly emphasize only two points:

First, the fast pace of our life places our minds and thinking under greater strain than ever before.

Second, our fast pace makes it even more imperative that we intentionally shape our mental habits into healthy ones. We have to build into our inner lives a haven where our hurried and over-burdened minds can find occasional respite.

We no longer have the luxury to stop, take time out, and reflect on a challenge or crisis. We are becoming more and more dependent on our reflexes to cope with the challenges that come our way. If we don't act immediately, we get left behind. This is true in every aspect of life, including the workplace, our families, and our marriages.

Spontaneous and automatic reactions are continually taking place around us. People don't take time to acquaint themselves with their inner thoughts. Maturity implies that we know how to counteract this impulsive way of responding by forming reflec-tive, not reflexive, habits—habits we can rely on when we feel we've reached the end of the rope.

A healthy response to an emergency is one in which we are able to draw on the total resources of the wonderful mind God has given us. That's what "habits of the mind" are all about. They automati-cally pop up when needed, allowing us to respond with mature reactions. In the long run, such habits not only avoid mistakes but help us to enjoy a more fulfilling and complete existence.

What Are Habits?

In his best-selling book *The Seven Habits of Highly Effective People*, Stephen Covey says that habits are powerful factors in our lives. "Because they are consistent, often unconscious patterns, they constantly, daily, express our character and produce our effec-tiveness . . . or ineffectiveness."[2]

Habits form the basis for our day-to-day responses to life. In fact, for its very survival, the structure of our society depends on the fact that people form habits. For instance, I drive the freeway to work each day. It's not a long drive but enough to demonstrate how important habits are to all of us. People, out of habit, stay in their lanes, indicate when they are going to move over, and avoid killing others. We call these habits "the rules of the road," but they must become habits before we are safe to use the roadway. Everything we learn ultimately becomes a habit.

Habits involve far more than the way we drive. I've come to recognize certain regulars by their private habits inside their cars as well. One lady has the habit of "putting on her face" while she drives to work. There's lots of stop-and-go in the morning commute, so she has plenty of time to apply her makeup. A man in a red sports car has the habit of eating his breakfast as he drives. He must love a certain fast-food place because his "breakfast-on-a-bun" and coffee cup always display the familiar golden arches. Another fellow shaves as he drives—electric razor of course.

All around us, habits reveal themselves. Take a few moments to observe yourself and those around you. Count the number of actions and reactions you see that clearly are habits of one sort or another. Unquestionably, habits dominate our lives.

Good and Bad Habits

There are both good habits and bad habits. Although my mother smoked incessantly, she always told me it was a bad habit and that I should never smoke. I never did. She died of lung cancer, verifying the fact that smoking is a dangerously bad habit. Tragically, however, she never stopped doing it.

Exercise is a good habit. I only wish I could be more obsessed with it. The trouble with good habits is they don't seem to stick as easily as bad habits. I wonder why?

Habits can be learned and unlearned. They are usually acquired over a lifetime of experience. As one habit is laid down, another begins to form on top of it creating a web of interdependent behaviors. There's little disagreement among the experts regarding that pattern. What is debatable is the extent to which habits can be broken. Good habits seem to be more easily removed while bad habits can be nearly impossible to get rid of.

Overall, however, I would say that all habits can be unlearned given the right motivation and opportunity. If I didn't believe this, I would have quit being a clinical psychologist a long time ago. I have seen people overcome the most horrible of habits and have learned that the very worst ones respond best to spiritual experiences and resources. We hardly ever break very bad habits through sheer will power. But with God's help, many alcoholics and drug or sexual addicts have found new beginnings, as they will gratefully tell you.

Covey very helpfully likens habits to the force of gravity. The gravity that might break a cherished vase when we accidentally drop it also keeps us in our car seats when we go around a sharp corner. In many powerful ways the force of gravity is our friend, helping keep the universe in order. Similarly, habits pull us toward a certain way of behaving or believing. Most times we are unaware that this force is operating until, of course, we try to remove it.

There is nothing wrong with gravity, just as there is nothing wrong with many habits. Gravity is a part of God's design for law and order. But unlearning habits can be like trying to achieve a liftoff into space by jumping in the air all by yourself. You will not escape the gravity of some habits without a tremendous amount of "special" power.

What Are Mental Habits?

Drug addictions, habits of anger, thumbsucking, and hair-pulling are all bad habits—but they have to do with conduct. Studying wisely is a good habit, along with cleanliness, debt-paying, and politeness (as I keep trying to tell my grandchildren).

However, habits don't always reveal themselves in behaviors. Habits can be thoughts—single thoughts or whole patterns of thought, good and bad. Sometimes those thoughts influence conduct, but often they merely shape our character and thrust us into unpleasant emotions.

This book isn't about behavior. I'm concerned here with whatever resides in that football-sized bony cage at the top of your body. The brain is the most marvelous, complex organ in all of the human body, and all habits are controlled by it. The pull of its mental habits is every bit as powerful as that of physical gravity.

There are many metaphors we can draw on for describing thought. Thoughts are tools that forge and shape our beliefs and will. Thoughts are poison that can sour the soul, destroy good intentions, or make you sick. But the metaphor I like best is that thoughts are seeds. They are planted in the garden of the mind, and if they are good seeds, they will bring forth much that is profitable. Thought seeds can make us happy or sad, ambitious or languid, hopeful or hopeless. If good seeds are planted in the right place, at the right time, and given the right care, they will bring good things to life.

The words of Paul in Galatians 6:7 are relevant here, when he reminds us that we reap what we sow. Farmers would agree, but there are not a lot of them around anymore to keep us aware of this agricultural truth. This verse primarily applies to our spiritual sowing and reaping—if we sow sin we will reap the products of sin. But sowing and reaping even goes beyond the spiritual and includes the physical and psychological. If we sow laziness and stress we will reap illness and a short life. If we sow bitterness and resentment we will reap misery and gloom. We can sum this up in a familiar phrase: cause and effect.

The analogy to seeds also helps to clarify that bad thoughts, or in garden parlance, "weeds," obey different laws from the seeds of good plants. By their very nature, weeds don't need care and cultivation. I've never yet met a gardener who said "Boy, I really had a job raising those weeds. It takes special green fingers." Weeds don't need raising; they raise themselves. And, in a mind left to itself, weed-thoughts will take over, thrive, perpetuate themselves, and destroy everything good in sight. Weeds are impossible to eradicate, except with painstaking hard work. So are bad mental habits.

Preparation for Good Habit Building

As we focus on the habits necessary to a healthy mind, let's first lay down some general principles that govern good habit formation. To begin with, it's important to make a distinction between dealing with sin in our lives and demolishing bad habits.

Not all bad habits are sinful, at least not directly sinful. Neglecting your body by not exercising is not in itself a sin—it is simply a bad habit. Furthermore, deliverance from sin is not deliverance from human nature, as Oswald Chambers rightly points out in the reading for September 8 in his book *My Utmost for His Highest*. In our context, we are talking about building good habits, not breaking sin patterns, though at times the distinction may not be all that clear-cut.

There are aspects to human nature, such as prejudices and bad traits, that are the result of flawed habits and neglect. God needs to change our disposition, not just deliver us from sin, in order to make us whole people. Some of us may well be effective in removing sin yet neglectful in our dealings with our dispositions. As you deal with changing your thought life, you will need to depend on God's power to help you. Furthermore, change will only come about if you agree to change. God does not force change on uncooperative participants.

Three Principles for Change

Having said that, let's consider some of the general principles for change that you'll need to attend to.

First, one of the best ways to eradicate a bad habit is to establish a new one that competes with the bad one. If the new, good habit is selected over the old, the old one will gradually be extinguished.

Second, creating a good habit requires a strong motivation for change. Simply having a desire for self-improvement isn't enough. Knowing what to do helps, but neither will that, by itself, get the job done, as every broken-New-Year's-resolution maker will attest. We all know what we should do, but that doesn't mean we do it.

Third, it's vital to stay motivated. How can you do this? Working together in a group provides the best incentive. Overwhelming research in the field of weight reduction, for example, has shown that the key to losing weight and keeping it off lies in having group support.[3] If you can persuade someone else to work with you, perhaps a friend or spouse, you will find it easier to keep up your motivation. Regular contact with others can encourage you, instruct you in changing, help you deal with failure, and enable you to avoid mistakes.

You'll also protect your motivation if you give yourself time to change. Nothing kills motivation like impatience. It is a well-known fact, for instance, that if you give up a substance like sugar or caffeine, your body takes twenty-one days to adjust. Before that time has passed, the body treats the change as an intruder. Only after twenty-one days is the change accepted as natural. There are obviously good reasons for this. The body thrives on stability, wants things to change as little as possible, and only adapts to the new situation slowly.

The twenty-one-day rule is pretty much good for all changes. When you've introduced a new habit or stopped an old one, let it go for at least twenty-one days so that the change can settle down. Don't expect it to become natural right away. For some, it might even take twice as long, so be patient.

You need to adopt the attitude of the marathon runner, not the sprinter. It is my observation that sprinters are naturally impulsive, whereas long-distance runners are patient and un-hurried. They know how to pace themselves, as illustrated in the fable of the tortoise and the hare. The tortoise won because he had the right attitude.

Motivation also survives better if you are flexible and build in some room for failure. Rigid programs of change fizzle pre-cisely because they are inflexible. A healthy mind is a mind that can tolerate setbacks then bounce back.

Rules for Building Strong Habits

How does one develop a habit? When it comes to forming bad habits, we usually don't have to think about them, because bad habits happen quite naturally. But good habits don't come that easily, so I've developed a summary of the essential rules for habit–building. You'll want to keep these rules in mind as you read the rest of this book:

Rule 1: Have a plan. No good habits can be formed without a plan, just as no beautiful garden can be shaped without a gardener's careful design. You must be intentional about what you intend to do.

Rule 2: Define the habit you desire. Spell out a specific definition for yourself. Make sure you write it down so that you can remind yourself of your intention.

Rule 3: Challenge whatever sabotages your new habit. Every garden has its pests. They need to be controlled or even eliminated. Think about what inhibits your habit and what aids it. If old friends keep dragging you down, avoid them for your own good. If certain circumstances trigger your failure, bypass those circumstances.

Rule 4: Set up a system of reminders. For a new habit to take root you need to have a system that can remind you to practice it. For example, notes on mirrors, in calendars, or on your car steering wheel can help keep you focused on your habit.

Rule 5: Reinforce your new habit. New habits need reinforcement—they must get their "rewards." Again, one of the strongest reinforcers is social approval. Ask a spouse or friend to praise and encourage you whenever you succeed. And reinforce yourself as well, remembering that God is saying, "Well done, good and faithful servant."

Rule 6: Change your plan if it isn't working. One important difference between a successful person and an unsuccessful person is that a successful person abandons plans that are not working and substitutes changes readily. This is true for successfully forming habits as well.

How the Ten Habits Fit Together

With those six rules in place, we are now ready to explore the thinking habits that are at the core of a healthy mind. I want to share with you the habits I have come to value after many years as a clinical psychologist and psychotherapist.

Figure 2 shows how I see them as a whole.

HOW THE TEN HABITS FIT TOGETHER

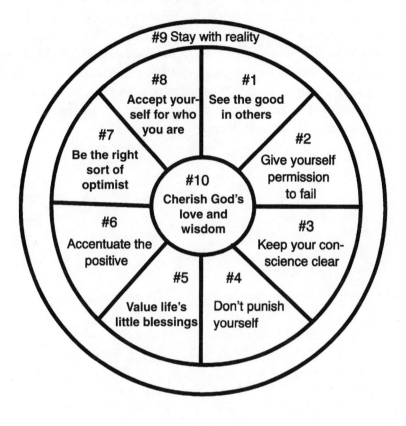

FIGURE 2

As you study this figure you will see that it takes the form of a wheel. At the center of the wheel is the tenth habit—*Cherish God's love and wisdom*. This is the hub around which all the other habits revolve. All thinking must resonate with God's wisdom if it is going to be healthy.

The outer rim is habit number nine—*Stay with reality*. This outer rim, or "tire" if you prefer, is where the rubber hits the road. All the habits must be united in reality, not fantasy or wishful thinking.

Between these two are the eight other habits making up the "spokes" of the wheel. If we are healthy thinkers, they will make the world go around for us.

As you review the ten habits, be on the lookout for others that might be important specifically for you, or develop variations that better suit your needs at this time. Keep notes of any alternative habits that might come to your mind as you read, then see how the principles of habit formation I will present can be applied to develop them. Move forward in this process with a mind and heart open to God's promptings, and I believe you will find a new level of peace and effectiveness in your life. In fact, I know you will. It's already happening for me.

THE TEN HABITS OF A HEALTHY MIND

As progressive and growing beings, we are all battered by outward circumstances that feel like they could destroy us. We easily come to believe that we have no control over these conditions. However, through right attitudes and godly beliefs we can squeeze out of these circumstances all the hidden good they have to offer. They can be our teachers not our tormentors.

In this section I will present the ten habits of the mind that I have found to be essential to my own spiritual and mental well-being. They are not exhaustive, but merely illustrative. My hope is that you will read these habits to discern what specific habits you need to consider for revitalizing your mental and spiritual hygiene.

CHAPTER 5

HABIT #1: SEE THE GOOD IN OTHERS

I am going to be meeting people today who talk too much—
people who are selfish, egotistical, ungrateful.
But I won't be surprised or disturbed
for I can't imagine a world without such people.
Roman Emperor Marcus Aurelius

O ld Madison Square Garden, New York's first indoor arena, was built in 1890. Crowning it, there once stood a statue of the goddess Diana. In Greek mythology Diana was a forest deity who later became an ardent huntress and patron of women, and the craftsman who sculptured the statue of Diana wanted to use a lovely girl for his model. He searched high and low and ultimately found someone who seemed to perfectly represent female beauty and grace. He duplicated her characteristics in his "Diana."

When the statue was finished and placed on the top of Madison Square Garden, it became an instant success. The statue was so beautiful that even the model became famous. Her beauty was stunning, and wherever she went, people recognized her as the model for Diana. She, like the statue, was applauded and acclaimed.

But fame rarely lasts, and personal tragedies soon befell the beautiful model. As time passed, her world collapsed. Ultimately, she became a derelict and a recluse.

Many years after the statue's first unveiling, a battered and homeless woman stumbled into a Salvation Army kitchen in a rundown New York City neighborhood. The woman begged for bread and soup. As she hungrily gulped down her food, the Salvation Army officer on duty watched her and puzzled over her appearance. Something about her seemed strangely familiar to him.

Finally, he asked her name. When she answered, he was amazed. His suspicions were confirmed. While everyone else saw a derelict, he saw someone with a special history. "You," he said to her, "are Diana."

A crooked smile, marred by several missing teeth, twisted across her face. Pleased by being recognized yet ashamed of what she had become, she quietly replied, "I *was* Diana."

What Do You See in Others?

This story was told by Og Mandino, a one-time derelict himself, who later became a leading author. When I first heard it, I was reminded of how easily people sometimes change for the worse. Life is fickle, and there are no guarantees for perpetual fame. We cannot hang on to the past, nor can we expect it to rescue us from life's terrible tragedies and disappointments.

But as I reflected further on the story, another key lesson finally settled in my mind. How readily the Salvation Army officer was able to see through the woman's outward appearance and recognize a person of bygone beauty and prestige! Every day that godly man encountered outcasts who had reached the pit of disgrace, who had been cast aside as society's dregs. Such daily exposure would be enough to harden even the gentlest of us. But not this man. He did not see bedraggled clothes. He did not see a careworn recluse. He did not see a depraved soul. He looked beyond the filth and discovered the beautiful Diana, a paragon of bygone beauty.

Every day of our lives we are given similar opportunities to see the good in other people, to discover their hidden magnificence or undisclosed beauty. There are a lot more "Dianas" around than we are willing to acknowledge. The greatest beauty of all is to be found inside people, if only we would take the trouble to look. Instead, however, we are inclined to notice the ragged edges of others' personalities or the ease with which they bristle when pushed too far. We humans are all inclined to overlook beauty when faced with evident imperfections.

Personal Likes and Dislikes

I have long pondered the way we develop personal likes and dislikes for people. Why is it that we so easily accept some people while we quickly develop a dislike for others, often without much cause either way? Furthermore, why is it that the majority of us have a strong tendency when meeting or interacting with certain people only to see the bad in them and never the good? Naturally, there are certain naive souls who are quite unable to discern the faults in others and are therefore easily conned by charm and appearance. But, in my experience, most of us are inclined to see the worst and not to expect the best.

I am particularly fascinated with first-impression likes and dislikes. After knowing individuals for a while, it's understandable that we should form an opinion about them. But why do we instinctively dislike someone we have never actually met or talked to? For me, it is a real puzzle.

As a youngster, I always dreaded advancing to the next grade level at school. The problem? What sort of teacher I would be getting, of course. Would she like me? Would I like her? We had very few male teachers in our school in my day, and we young boys never really got comfortable with our women teachers. We confused them with our mothers if they were older and fell madly in love with them if they were younger.

Before many years had passed, I discovered that my first impressions were always wrong. When I liked someone, she turned out to be a teacher from hell. When I disliked someone, she turned out to be kind, loving, and long-suffering. It became so predictable that, after a few years, I came to believe that the best reaction I could have to a new teacher was to immediately dislike her!

These observations can only lead to one conclusion—we should make it a habit to *always* see the good in others, and I mean *always*. This rule should apply not only to first impressions, but to lifelong relationships as well. Don't trust your second, or third, or any impressions. Always try to look for some good in everyone, no matter how obnoxious they appear at any given moment.

This is not only a healthy habit, it is what God expects of us. In John 15:12 Jesus tells His disciples, "This is my commandment, That ye love one another, as I have loved you." Seeing the good in others has nothing to do with liking, but everything to do with loving.

Liking Versus Loving

Will Rogers, the cowboy humorist, first uttered the now famous words: "I never met a man I didn't like." I don't know whether to believe him or not. Did he really mean never? I don't think we can be expected to like everyone we meet—it's impossible. God has created some very strange people (I might even be one of them myself!). Yet you and I are expected to love everyone. And there is a vast difference between liking and loving.

There are many reasons why we like or dislike certain people, and often the reasons we give are not the real reasons. For instance, we might believe that we like a neighbor because he is cheerful. Then we remember that we disliked someone else because she was cheerful and we often wished she would wipe that stupid grin off her face. While there are many reasons we might like a particular person, most of our liking is too mysterious to be defined or predicted.

Because liking is so capricious, God removes it from consideration in His kingdom. He doesn't put much store by our likes and dislikes—they are simply irrelevant when it comes to how we should relate to one another in the body of Christ. In fact, nowhere in Scripture does God command us to like anyone. What He requires is for us to love one another.

Of course, loving is no easier than liking. In fact it is harder. Loving galls our natural instincts. We would much prefer to annihilate some people or at least hope they fall flat on their faces. Fortunately, God loves the people we don't like and seems to be able to use them, despite our disapproval.

This truth comes out most starkly when you examine those Scriptures that tell us to "love our enemies" (Matt. 5:44). We are required by God to accept people for what they are: the good, the bad, and the ugly. It is precisely because we don't like some people that God has provided us with the capacity to love them. In reality, if we liked them we wouldn't need the admonition to love them.

The habit I am advocating here involves setting aside our likes or dislikes, and placing judgment on hold. If we like someone, we have a bonus, but real love is intended for those we don't like. This is the genius of our capacity, as Christians, to love. Christian love is designed to overcome our dislikes, even our hatreds and fears. Why else is Christian love, as defined in the thirteenth chapter of 1 Corinthians, such a powerful force in our world?

Not Everyone Likes Me Either

It helps me to remember that, just as I don't like everyone I meet, not everyone likes me either. Reminding ourselves of that unpleasant little truth can help straighten out our thinking. But this realization often eludes us. We are always surprised when we find that someone dislikes us.

The best antidote for being disliked is to love back anyway and to search for the good in the other person. We can then foster that good into a robust, loving response. Whether your feelings change isn't important. You may spend the rest of your life disliking someone, but you will benefit from the antidote in reduced unhappiness, irritability, and vain regret. And the truth is, if you focus on loving and seeing the good in others, your feelings *will* begin to change. You will stop being overly sensitive, no longer obsessed with how you are perceived. You will begin to care about others in a new way. Right behavior and thinking always result in right feelings.

An Inaccurate First Impression

Sometimes our dislike of someone does not come from a first impression. It may be reinforced by second, third, and even tenth impressions. This makes no difference in the habit I am advocating here, except to make the task a little harder.

The first year of my marriage to my beautiful wife, Kathleen, I took a job as a newly graduated engineer in a city 350 miles from where the two of us had grown up. We rented an apartment in a ten-unit complex, and we lived in the center of the second floor. At one end of our floor lived a couple with two small children. We liked the man, but from the outset both Kathleen and I took a dislike to the woman. She was tall and imposing and seemed cold and aloof. She never greeted us unless we greeted her first.

Both Kathleen and I had a British-type upbringing, and we understood the reserve often associated with it. But this was somehow different and far more intimidating. This woman's frosty style frightened us youngsters, living all alone in a new part of South Africa.

Months passed. Kathleen, who desperately wanted to have a baby, began to have a series of miscarriages. She seemed unable to keep a baby in her womb longer than the first three months, and consequently she became desperate and very despondent. All this time we avoided "Mrs. Coldness" down the corridor. We didn't think she could understand what we were feeling.

Finally, after some treatment, a pregnancy took. Then, in about the seventh month, Kathleen began to bleed and have pains. The doctor put her to bed and tried some medication to stabilize the pregnancy, but after a few weeks it aborted. The baby's head was greatly swollen because of hydrocephalus. I was bewildered; Kathleen was devastated. It felt like the end of the world. Would we ever be able to have a baby?

It was then that the lady we disliked so much stepped in and became a ministering angel.

The woman had once been a nurse and knew exactly what to do. In order for me to return to work, she took over the daytime nursing of Kathleen, who had become poisoned by the dead fetus. Every evening, she prepared a meal for us. Kindness overflowed everywhere, and inevitably, we came to like and respect her. Eventually we learned that the woman's aloofness was nothing more than a profound shyness from which she had suffered all her life. When she was needed, she was able to set her modesty and reserve aside, revealing a totally different person. We had only seen the cold side of her. The warm side won our hearts.

Now, I suppose we could blame people like her for having two natures. But until such time as the world is perfect, who are we to judge others for having two sides and only showing us one? Make a habit of searching for the good side in others, and even if they turn out to have two bad sides, you will still be the beneficiary of your habit. Seeing the good in others makes you a nicer person, far easier to love. As Norman Vincent Peale once said, getting people to like you is the other side of your liking them.

The Divine Formula

It's important to remember that God has not abandoned us to overcome our dislikes all by ourselves. He can give us the desire and capacity to change how we perceive others. What He does not give us is the right to ask others to change before we are willing to love them.

Sad to say, millions of Christians operate this way, and it is particularly evident between husbands or wives. "If you'd just change, I'd be able to love you again." I've heard this from scores of men and women. Perhaps there is an important reason why an unkind wife or an unfaithful husband should change, but to make that change a condition violates the foundation for real love.

God didn't ask us to change before He could love us. He loved us first, and as a result gave us the power to change. Likewise, if people are to change, it is most likely to happen because we love them first. They may be thoroughly unlikable in their present state, and the love we offer may have to be tough love. But change will happen a lot sooner if we do not make it a condition for our love.

Four Key Steps

So what does it take to see the good side of others? Keep these four principles in mind.

Principle 1: Acknowledge your own unloveliness. We all have an unlovely side, which causes others to dislike us from time to time. Remembering this humbles us and reminds us not to judge others for being unlovely and unlikable.

Principle 2: Set aside emotional reactions. We needn't be controlled by our likes or dislikes. We can choose to overlook bad feelings.

Principle 3: Remember that every person is loved by God. When you are faced with unlikable people, imagine Christ taking them in His arms, drawing them close to His bosom, and loving them. He then turns to you and says, "Do the same, My child."

Principle 4: Recognize your own need to be seen as a good person. By reminding ourselves that we want others to love us, we are able to overcome our faulty thinking. This motivates us to do the right thing, although we may not always get it right.

God honors right motives, even if our actions are wrong. If we fail hopelessly in trying to see the good in others, the blessing is in the trying. Success is merely a bonus. And that very important point brings us to our next healthy habit: giving ourselves permission to fail.

CHAPTER 6

Habit #2:
Give Yourself Permission to Fail

We need to teach the highly educated person
that it is not a disgrace to fail and that he must
analyze every failure to find its cause.
He must learn to fail intelligently,
for failing is one of the greatest arts in the world.
Charles Kettering (renowned inventor)

In the movie *The Best of Times*, Robin Williams stars as a man who cannot accept failure. Twenty years before, his high–school football team lost an important game because he dropped the ball, and he was never able to forget it. Subsequently, that football failure became an obsession. If only he could undo the past! He devised a way to do so—he decided to recreate the game and give himself a second chance at success.

In the course of the story, Williams persuades the members of both teams to come to a reunion where they have a rematch. Well, you can imagine the rest—it could only happen in the movies. In the re–created game, at the critical moment in the final play, the ball is passed to Williams. This time he makes the catch and re-deems his failure.

Wouldn't life be wonderful if we all could get second chances like that? I've dropped a few passes along the way and would love a chance for a replay. They weren't football passes either—most of my dropped passes have had to do with relationships. All but one.

My Personal Failure

Fortunately my failures have not been too numerous. But a particular, horrendous situation still stands out in my mind. At the time it happened, it totally devastated me. Later on, it turned out to be one of God's greatest gifts to me. And that is my point—in the final analysis, there is really no such thing as failure in God's kingdom—only "forced growth." For this reason, we needn't fear failure as much as we do.

Giving yourself permission to fail does not mean that you don't care about succeeding. Of course we want to succeed. We should always examine whether or not we are trying our best and giving all we've got to overcome the challenge facing us. But commitment to excellence and fear of failure are two entirely different things.

A well-adjusted person is able to confront failure without its becoming a catastrophe. He or she knows that it is not the end of the world. Claiming the freedom to fail is vital to ultimate success, because, as any successful person will tell you, success is nothing more than failure with the "garbage brushed off."

My noteworthy failure happened when I was in my late twenties. In my first career I was a civil engineer, and in some respects I was an ideal engineering candidate because of my talent and interest. After my conversion, I had toyed with the idea of pastoring or missionary work, but that could come later. After all, the skills of a civil engineer are highly desirable in underdeveloped countries.

Once I qualified as an engineer, Kathleen and I married and moved to a beautiful city in the Natal province of South Africa. I was quite successful and achieved rapid promotions. However, I felt the need for additional study in mathematics, so I enrolled in a part-time course.

I studied for an entire year, more or less neglecting my family but promising them it would soon be over. My employer even paid for the studies and gave me time off. At the end of the year I went in to take the university examination. If I passed I would get credit for the year's work. If I failed it would mean redoing the whole course. Needless to say, I was quite nervous.

I opened the examination envelope and began to work on the first problem. Now you must understand that I had considered myself to be quite a math whiz, receiving top marks and even winning a prize for mathematics achievement at the end of high school. So when the problem I was working on started going nowhere, I began to panic. I quickly moved to the next problem. "Cut your losses and move on" had always been my examination strategy; at least it had always worked in the past.

I didn't fare so well with the next problem, either. By now I was sweating profusely. I had never failed an examination in my life. What was going wrong? After repeated attempts at other questions, I could take it no longer. I got up, handed in the incomplete examination book, and left in disgrace. For the first time in my life I had failed an examination, and I didn't know how to handle it.

For weeks I was depressed. A year of my life had been wasted, my self-confidence was shaken, and my future as a great engineer had capsized. This was to be my "moment of breaking," as M. Scott Peck calls it, a moment when all dependence on your own self-sufficiency is shattered. You stare at the stark reality that you can't win all the time. Sometimes you simply lose.

My wife was forgiving, my boss was forgiving, but I couldn't forgive myself. Slowly I began to recover, but for quite a while I had no ambition and could not envision the future. All I could see was that one appalling failure. I punished myself ruthlessly for it.

My greatest struggle was with how to understand this failure in the context of my Christian experience. What was God doing? Had He caused this to happen? Was He punishing me? How should I, as a Christian, receive such an experience, and how could I integrate it with my faith? For many months these questions were to be my obsession. I'll tell you more about the answers I received a little later.

Everyone Feels Failure's Arrows

I have given a lot of thought over the years to the problem of failures and why they devastate us. First of all, they happen to everyone simply because we're human. We make mistakes. Others make mistakes and we suffer disappointments, no matter how hard we try to keep our expectations in check.

We don't even have to actually fail at something in order to feel like a failure. Just have people reject you because you don't give them want they want, and you'll feel like you have failed them. Amazing, isn't it? You don't get chosen for the team. You find yourself overlooked for a promotion. Worse still, your spouse rejects you and demands a divorce. These, and many other life experiences, are fraught with potential for failure feelings, even when we haven't done anything wrong. There is no way to escape feeling as if we've failed. The big question then, is: What do we do with genuine failure?

Where are we to go with our disappointments? Even in our Christian subculture, we see people all around us who are driven to seek success but have no idea what role failure plays in building success. They don't know how to receive it with grace. They are unable to incorporate it into their Christian experience. The church has, by and large, uncritically fostered a theology of success. In contrast, it has no theology of failure. If anything, failure is viewed as something no Christian should have to deal with. This has left many of the faithful believing that if they fail, it is simply because God has turned His back on them.

This is exactly what a patient said to me recently. He had come to believe, through the teaching of his pastor, that if God's presence and blessing are truly in your life, you will be successful. Now, facing bankruptcy in his business, he fears that God is displeased with him. Never in his ten years as a Christian did anyone even hint at the possibility that sometimes God speaks loudest through our apparent failures.

The truth is, most people who have succeeded at something great have built their success upon a mountain of failure. This led one prominent businessman to say, "The way to accelerate your success is to double your failure rate." Of course we don't intentionally seek out failure; it just happens. And it usually gives us a second chance—to fail again.

Why Does Failure Devastate Us?

We live in a success–driven culture. In fact, one could say that success is our national religion. Many Christians have made an idol of it. We have created a myth that asserts that God only desires our success. What a lie! God is not in the success business but in the refining business. What He desires is our sanctification, our purification. His Word verifies this: "But he knoweth the way that I take: when he hath tried me, I shall come forth as gold" (Job 23:10).

Another passage says much the same thing. "That the trial of your faith, being much more precious than of gold that perisheth, though it be tried with fire, might be found unto praise and honor and glory at the appearing of Jesus Christ" (1 Pet. 1:7).

If we know in our hearts that God uses failure to refine us, why does failure devastate us? Mainly because we do not understand its role in God's purification program. There are other reasons too.

1. *Failure devastates us because it points out our imperfections.* I thought I was a math whiz. I had never before had difficulty with even the most complex math concepts and believed myself to have an intuitive grasp of mathematics. After that ill-fated exam, I realized it was all a delusion. Even though I had studied hard, my imperfection was real. And I didn't like it!

2. *Failure devastates us because we irrationally confuse FAILING with being a FAILURE.* I may fail a lot, but it doesn't make me a failure. You are not a failure just because you fail, but you are a failure when you quit trying. As Steve Davis puts it, "It may not be your fault for getting down, but it has got to be your fault for not getting up."

When Is Failure Not a Failure?

Don't you love those stories about people who seem to have failed, and then it turns out that they haven't failed at all? For a start, consider the life of Christ. Humanly speaking, His life was a total catastrophe. What with dying a criminal's death on a cross, and so young, His story isn't exactly the stuff of which a success manual is made.

The August 5 reading from *My Utmost for His Highest* by Oswald Chambers has always stuck in my mind. "God," Chambers writes, "called Jesus Christ to what seemed unmitigated disaster." From a human standpoint, the life of Jesus was an absolute failure. But from God's viewpoint it was a tremendous triumph because it fulfilled His perfect plan for the world. Success or failure is just a matter of perspective. Consider the following true stories:

There once was a boy who suffered from terrible depression throughout most of his early life. Although born into the aristocracy, he was virtually neglected by his parents and was raised by his nanny. He was teased mercilessly by his peers for having a ponderous head and being clumsy. He failed the sixth grade, and at sixteen was sent home from Harrow, his prestigious boarding school, with a report card that said, "This young man shows a conspicuous lack of success."

Years later that boy, by then the prime minister of England in charge of defending the British Empire against Hitler, would chuckle over that misplaced judgment. His name? Sir Winston Churchill—probably the finest leader England has ever had. But it took a lifetime of failures to bring him to his—and England's—finest hour.

A young German university student of Jewish descent finished his Ph.D. dissertation and submitted it to the University of Bern. It came back with these words scrawled across it by his professor: "This thesis is irrelevant and fanciful." Rather than being devastated and throwing in the towel, he picked up the pieces of his life and took his dissertation to another university, the University of Zurich. He became one of the greatest physicists ever—Albert Einstein. And it was the University of Zurich who recognized his talents and gave him a position as a junior professor. Was his rejection a failure? Apparently not.

A mother in Ohio once received a visit from the local schoolmaster of the village school. He told her that her boy really had no great mental ability and suggested that she put him to work on the farm. He would never benefit from his intellect. The mother refused and home-schooled him.

Later in life he wrote these words: "When everybody else is quitting on a problem, that is the time to begin." He signed it "Thomas A. Edison," a man known today as a genius in the practical application of scientific principles. Edison invented the telephone, the incandescent lamp, and the electric train. We owe him thanks for the movies, synthetic rubber, and thirteen hundred other patents. The boy who had no intellect became the world's greatest inventor. So much for failure.

Another young man, brought up in the highlands of Scotland, went to seminary so he could become a minister. He was assigned to preach his first sermon in a country church near the seminary. Standing in the high pulpit of the Church of Scotland, he opened his Bible when the time came to preach and promptly forgot his text. In great humiliation he fled from the pulpit crying out, "I am a total failure. I will never preach again."

About twenty-five years ago, before I came to the United States, I was sent to central Africa to interview engineers who were departing that region and seeking positions down south. The hotel where I was conducting the interviews was right on the banks of the mighty Zambezi River, close to Victoria Falls. During a break in the interviews I took a walk through the bush, past wild animals, to the edge of the falls. What a sight! The thick mist and roar of the mighty falls can be seen and heard for twenty-five miles around.

Alongside the falls stands the statue of the preacher who forgot his text; the statue placed directly in line with the face of the falls he discovered in 1855. His name appears in large letters at the base of the huge statue: David Livingston. Was his faulty memory a failure? No way. Just a little correction to a lifelong trajectory.

Was My Failure a Failure?

Some months after having failed my math exam so horribly, I was paging through the university catalog and my eyes fell on some courses that were being offered in psychology. Suddenly my heart started to race. Something warmed inside of me. I had recently tried to help some troubled young people at our church, and now it dawned on me that I could be a lot more effective if I knew a little more about people and their pain.

A strong conviction gripped me that God was calling me to some special form of ministry. I didn't know what it was, but I was resonating with something new. My sense of purpose was being restored. The next day I sent off an application that would get me started in my first psychology course. Later, I would focus on clinical psychology.

Over the years God has brought me into contact with many emotionally troubled Christians. I was appalled at how little, if any, Bible–based psychological help there was available for them. The church seemed to have turned its back on these hurting souls. The few psychiatrists and psychologists I knew were all blatant agnostics, a fashionable philosophy in their profession.

At that stage, apart from the writings of the Christian Swiss psychiatrist Paul Tournier, I'd never even heard of anyone in clinical psychology or psychiatry who was a devout believer. Nonetheless, I knew that I had to proceed in this direction. I never had a clue where it would take me, but it didn't matter. I have never, before or since, felt the pressure of God more strongly than at that time in my life.

As I reflect back on my devastating experience in that examination room all those years ago, I have to ask myself this question: Was it really a failure? Or was God's compassionate and all-knowing hand upon my life nudging me in another direction? Through it came a totally new assignment, and the rest of the story is obvious. How grateful I am to God for the opportunities I have since had to minister to hurting people, especially pastors.

I say again with all the sincerity I can muster, in God's kingdom there is no such thing as failure, and today I give myself permission to fail. I don't seek it. I certainly smart from it. Yet there is a part of me that jumps with excitement when I look into the eyes of defeat or disappointment. Who knows what destiny lies beyond the disappointment, what new direction is to follow? Whatever it is, I've learned to see failure as a disguise for God's best plan for my life. I invite you to do the same.

CHAPTER 7

HABIT #3: KEEP YOUR CONSCIENCE CLEAR

A person's conscience ain't got no sense,
and it just goes for him anyway . . .
It takes up more room than all the rest of a person's
insides, and yet ain't no good, no how.
Huck in *Huckleberry Finn* (Mark Twain)

Let me be absolutely honest here—this is one of the hardest habits to cultivate. No emotion is more prone to distortion than our built-in sense of knowing right from wrong. Conscience can take us by the hand and lead us to God. In fact, the Holy Spirit's conviction works through our conscience, and there is clearly a connection between God's conviction and our conscience.

On the other hand, the thing we call conscience can be a real tyrant. It is always ready to condemn us. Once it gets our scent, it will hound us mercilessly. Worse yet, when feelings of guilt—true or false—are pushed out of our awareness, they become festering emotional sores. Unresolved guilt can cause nervous breakdowns, stress disease, psychosomatic illnesses, and abject misery.

So is conscience a reliable voice? Shakespeare explored the subject a long time ago, and several times in *Richard III* he refers to it. Queen Margaret says, "Conscience . . . the worm . . . that begnaws the soul."

King Richard says, "My conscience hath a thousand several tongues, and every tongue brings in a several tale, and every tale condemns me for a villain."

Conscience is rarely consistent or rational. When it speaks, you can never be sure whether it is telling the truth or presenting a pack of lies. Even when conscience is truthful, it seldom lets you off lightly. It will denounce you for being a villain and thrust you into abject distress to pay for your errors, whether those errors are real or imagined.

A Useless Emotion?

Although most secular psychologists see guilt as a useless emotion, I disagree. I don't think any form of civilization can survive without the restraint that conscience provides. It certainly wouldn't be safe to live in such a society, and the eventual outcome of several notable examples are well recorded in history.

Conscience has the potential for warping and torturing the human mind, but it also makes us pay our bills and honor our promises. No one in his or her right mind should want to live without a conscience. In fact, we have a name for those who do—we call them sociopaths.

There are many situations in which a feeling of guilt is appropriate and necessary. Perhaps we have hurt someone. We have violated their rights and need to take responsibility for our actions. I call this "true" or healthy guilt. True guilt seeks to put matters right, to make amends, to give and receive forgiveness. It's important for us to do everything in our power to discern that what we're feeling is a true guilt.

When conscience condemns us for petty things, we refer to it as "false" guilt. False guilt saps our energy and diverts us from productive living because it robs us of any good and happy feelings we might have. It poisons our relationships, stifles our initiative, and inhibits our growth. We become stunted, immature, and unable to be ourselves authentically. This happens because false guilt distorts our sense of wrongdoing. When secular psychologists condemn guilt as the "useless emotion," it is this form of guilt they are referring to.

False guilt is what we feel when no actual violation has occurred, when we exaggerate some petty mistake we've made, or when we refuse to forgive ourselves even though we have been forgiven. False guilt tortures our mind. Its goal is to make us miserable. If your conscience is neither truthful nor able to receive forgiveness, you have some work to do in getting it back on a healthy track.

When Guilt Distorts

We need look no further than the Bible for evidence that the conscience can become distorted. Nowhere in Scripture is the conscience presented as our only source of moral information. In fact, the contrary is true. Scripture warns us that the "conscience being weak is defiled" (1 Cor. 8:7), that it can be "seared with a hot iron" (1 Tim. 4:2) and that one's heart can be "sprinkled from an evil conscience" (Heb. 10:22). These are all references to a distorted conscience.

Scripture, however also tells us that we can have "a good conscience" (1 Pet. 3:16), and it is this "good conscience" that is our goal here. Our spiritual ears need to be finely tuned to the tiniest whisper of God's voice rather than to the unreliable, confusing messages that continuously babble within our minds.

A Case of Distorted False Guilt

In therapy, I once saw a father who was on the verge of taking his life to appease his distorted conscience. It was one of the saddest cases I have ever dealt with in all my years as a clinical psychologist. And it illustrates many of the points I want to make about guilt.

Sam came to see me at his wife's insistence. Life had become so miserable for the whole family that she was considering leaving him, and it was the threat of being abandoned by his family that finally convinced him that he needed help. When I first saw him, Sam was utterly despondent. If I had prescribed a physical remedy for his guilt, such as demanding that he crawl around the world on hands and knees, he would have gladly done it. Like a savage cancer guilt was eating him up.

Sam's difficulties had begun some years before. An avid boat builder, he loved crafting boats of all types—rowing boats, sailing boats, or small power boats. Because he could only use one boat for himself at a time, he helped other people build boats too. His workshop teemed with activity as a steady stream of friends shared the gift of Sam's nautical skill and enthusiasm.

One day Sam decided to build himself a new boat. His five-year-old son became involved, as young boys do, by getting in the way, messing in the glue, and misplacing tools. But for Sam this was part of the fun. He knew he was passing on a valuable skill to his son. The day came when the boat was finished and father and son were ready to launch it in a local lake. "Make sure you take life preservers with you," his wife warned him.

"I'm only going to test the boat, not sail to Hawaii," Sam replied sarcastically. "Why," he mumbled to himself, "does she always have to nag? I know what I'm doing!"

Sam put his young son in the new boat without a life preserver. He launched it, and breaking his promise to stay in shallow water, he allowed the boat to float into a deeper part of the lake. He was so preoccupied with locating a small leak in the front that he didn't pay attention to his son's antics at the back of the boat. Moments later he noticed that the boy was missing. He panicked and tried to retrace the path the boat had covered. Ten minutes later, he found his little son trapped under the water in some reeds. It was too late to revive him.

The Tyranny of Neurotic Guilt

From that moment, Sam began to change for the worse. After the funeral he became a recluse. He wallowed in self-pity. He became obsessed with two strong beliefs. First, he was the cause of his son's death. Second, God was punishing him for some sin from his past. Sam's mind was submerged in abject torment.

The first belief was at least partially true and could not be sidestepped. His neglect had contributed to his son's death. No child should ever be allowed to get into a boat without a life preserver. But as painful as this was to Sam, I think he could have accepted reality and moved forward.

It was the second belief, the really destructive one, that was to be his undoing. There is no fear more debilitating than the fear that when something bad happens God is punishing us. I think all of us have some tendency toward such a belief. I'd like to think this comes about more because of what our preachers *don't* say than because of what they *do* say. However, I have heard some pretty horrible stories about what believers have been taught in this regard.

Harold Kushner, in his marvelous book *When Bad Things Happen to Good People*, explains why this belief is so tempting. When bad things happen to good people, he says, they believe that God is a righteous judge who gives them exactly what they deserve. This is one of the ways people try to make sense of the world.

Sam could not shake this idea. "God is punishing me, and that's all there is to understand," he would say to me. Case closed.

Is Guilt God's Punishment?

Was Sam right? Is it true that bad things are God's punishment? After all, He allows them to happen. If He is supposed to be in charge of everything and something bad occurs, He must have meant for it to happen.

Of course Sam was wrong. But this issue raises a more generic question, one we need to resolve if we are going to have a healthy conscience. Does God punish us at all on this side of eternity? If He does, what does this say about grace? If I am to be punished for my sin now, why do I need the forgiveness of the cross? One cannot have it both ways. Either one is punished or one is forgiven!

Unless we get our theology straight, we can never achieve a clear conscience. Sound theology never gets us into trouble. Bad theology is devastating and is always an obstacle to developing a healthy mind. What then is the correct way of understanding how God deals with us?

First of all, it is true that God disciplines us. He allows things to happen so that we can learn from our mistakes, and He doesn't rush in to fix all our indiscretions. Scripture calls it chastening. "For whom the Lord loveth he chasteneth," says Hebrews 12:6.

But this is different from punishment. Discipline teaches us to be more responsible. God allows us to suffer natural consequences as a way of instructing us to be more accountable. Much of God's chastening isn't what He does to us, but is what He doesn't rescue us from.

My grandchildren are quickly learning that God does not rescue them, nor do their good parents, when they don't do their homework. We reap what we sow, so be prepared to reap whatever harvest your neglect and bad behavior sows. God is far more likely to rescue us from circumstances we haven't sown.

Second, yes, God does punish people, but His punishment is reserved for the Judgment Day. God's punishment is different from His chastisement. It is a penalty. It settles a debt that we owe. Once we are punished, we don't owe anyone anything anymore. As Christians, we believe that Jesus Christ paid the penalty for our sins when He died on the cross. Because of His sacrifice, the debt is canceled.

So, does God punish us anyway? Does He settle His account with us by allowing some disaster to befall us in life? I believe not. Such an idea doesn't make theological sense.

And in Sam's case an even more puzzling question emerges: Why would God punish someone else for Sam's sin? Did God kill a young boy because the father sinned? What did the boy do to deserve the death penalty on behalf of his father? Did he die so that his father could be punished? It makes a mockery of God's gift of grace. Only one Son died for our sins, and it wasn't Sam's.

Do you see how an erroneous theology can be the cause of serious emotional problems? The only way those of us beset by a destructive conscience can become healthy again is to follow God's plan of salvation: Rely on Christ to pay all the debt for all your sin. Stop blaming God for your mistakes, and stop punishing yourself as a way of trying to appease God.

Darkness before the Dawn

Sam was to discover that it is darkest just before morning light. Because of his distorted beliefs about God's punishment, the poor man turned to alcohol, became a binge drinker, skipped work, and even turned to gambling as a way of distracting himself from his misery. He could not bring himself to forgive his carelessness, and he was furious at God for punishing him.

Regrettably, his emotional distress was so deep and pervasive that Sam's wife did leave him for a while. She did so partly because she blamed him for the accident but mostly because she could not live with his tormented mind. Sam was compounding his self-destruction by piling pain upon pain.

When I first started therapy with Sam, he vividly described his inner voice of guilt as blaming him constantly for his irresponsibility. "It's sometimes soft and mocking. Other times it screams at me so that I feel my head wants to burst," he explained. He was not talking about an auditory hallucination. He was referring to the voice of conscience, a voice that speaks to all of us through our own self-talk.

While intense feelings of guilt are sometimes resistant to therapy, Sam did begin to turn things around. We spent quite a bit of time examining his irrational beliefs as they were expressed in his distorted theological ideas. He had to learn that he, not God, was doing the punishing. God was offering him forgiveness freely and generously. It was Sam who had turned his back on God, accusing Him of not rescuing his son and thus refusing to take responsibility for his neglect.

Slowly he came to understand. Eventually his wife joined us in therapy, and the marriage was saved. This is not to say that Sam was totally released from his memories and pain. That would take a long time. But he was now headed in the right direction, no longer sabotaging the healing process.

Petty Guilt Is All Around Us

Sam's story is not a commonplace one. It does, however, show how conscience can become a tyrant. It certainly illustrates the steps necessary for disabling a monster conscience.

Tragedies are few and far between, and most guilt problems of ordinary folk fall into the category of petty. We generally suffer from guilt over exaggerated or imagined violations. The conscience with the real problem is not one that makes a big deal over a serious violation. It is the conscience that kicks up a fuss over petty infractions, even unreal sin. Such a conscience is just as much a tyrant as Sam's. In a word, we call such a conscience neurotic. It is a sign that something has gone wrong with our guilt system.

This is not the place for me to go into the many reasons why a conscience goes off the rails and becomes so unreliable. Needless to say, it has a lot to do with our upbringing and the culture in which we live, which is by and large a punitive one. Someone must always be blamed when something goes wrong.

In any case, neurotic guilt is all around us, even within us. Suppose someone asks me to speak at a conference or to preach at a church. I know I am already overcommitted and should refuse. But when I say no I feel terribly guilty. Why? Isn't it my right to say no? Of course it is. Then why do I feel so guilty when I do? The answer is easy—I've been taught to feel this way.

Perhaps one of my children or grandchildren wants something and asks me to buy it for him or her. I know it is a bit of a luxury and not really necessary. I don't really have the money to buy what they want, so I refuse. Do I feel good? No, I feel lousy. My guilt buttons have been pushed, and my failure to comply gives me no peace, even though I know I did the right thing.

We feel guilty when someone snubs us, fearing that we may have done something to deserve it. We feel guilty for not telephoning our parents. Children feel guilty for doing what their parents told them not to do, students for not reading their assignments, and restaurant cooks for not giving their customers value for money. I will refrain from making any comments about how hard it must be to be used-car salesmen. How do they feel when they sell a lemon to an unsuspecting customer?

Whatever other habits we form, we need to develop the habit of maintaining a clear conscience. This requires that we learn how to recognize healthy, or true, guilt and apply the right remedy. It also means we should recognize petty, or sick, guilt and dispose of it as quickly as possible. This may be a tall order, but I believe it is possible.

How to Tell True from False Guilt

As we've already noted, there are times when guilt is appropriate and necessary. If we've done something wrong, we need a warning signal to direct us toward corrective action. True guilt serves as a flashing red indicator light. But how can we know whether it is a real concern? For it to be true guilt the following criteria must be met:

1. *The feeling of guilt must be linked to a real, and not imagined, violation.* The complicating factor in Sam's story is that he could not sort out his real culpability from his imagined fault. He needed to feel some guilt over his carelessness, but the guilt he felt because he believed God was punishing him was out of the bounds of reality. We receive forgiveness and heal our minds when we acknowledge real guilt, and the case is closed.

The point to remember here is this: Only true guilt can be forgiven. False guilt, the guilt we feel over imagined violations, is neurotic precisely because it cannot be forgiven. There is nothing to forgive.

2. *The feeling of guilt must be appropriately proportioned to the violation.* When I inadvertently bump an old person in the supermarket so that he drops and breaks a bottle of ketchup, there is an appropriate feeling of guilt that should follow my carelessness. But how much? Is it normal if I lose a whole night's sleep over it? Obviously not. It should be enough to force me to apologize and pay for the broken bottle. Beyond this, guilt is false and neurotic. On the other hand, if I cheat on my income tax, it might be appropriate for me to lose a few nights' sleep until I put matters right—whether I'm caught or not.

The point is, the feeling of guilt should always match the seriousness of the violation.

Healing False Guilt

When we are forgiven for true guilt, by God or someone else, we should be released from guilt feelings. But herein lies a real challenge. Even when we've been forgiven, the feeling of guilt is often perpetuated. When this happens, false guilt takes advantage of true guilt to exert its domination and to sabotage our happiness.

What is one to do about these feelings? There is only one thing to do: *ignore them*. There is little else we can do to take our neurotic feelings away. No pills are available. No amount of penance will suffice. This kind of guilt is totally neurotic. You can, however, reason with it in your self-talk. Allow me to illustrate with a personal example.

As a new Christian in my late teens, studying to be an engineer, I had to travel to Johannesburg by commuter train to go to classes at the university. One day, being early, I took a walk up the main street of the city to kill time and passed a beggar sitting against a shop window. He greeted me and asked for money. I could see that he was hungry.

I had the equivalent of a quarter in my pocket, and that was all. Should I give it to the beggar? I intended to use the money to buy a meat pie for my dinner as I would be working late in the electrical lab. "No," I said to myself, "I must keep it for myself, or I'll be hungry later and I won't be able to concentrate."

I walked on. But, with growing alarm, I felt as if God were convicting me and telling me to give the money to the beggar. I walked further. Eventually, I was so overcome with guilt that I turned around and ran as fast as I could back to where the beggar was sitting. He wasn't there anymore. He seemed to have vanished into thin air. I was puzzled. If God had been convicting me, then why didn't He cause the beggar to wait there so I could give him my dinner money? Sure, I had delayed, but I had responded.

Now I felt even worse. When dinner time came I couldn't bring myself to spend the money. I felt too guilty and puzzled over what God was doing. Did God really convict me, or was this just my neurotic stuff coming out? I did not know; I was too young in the faith. I felt terrible.

After a couple of hours of self-imposed misery I decided that it wasn't God who was convicting me at all; it was my own conscience. So I resolved just to "step over my guilt," just to ignore it as I would any physical object in my path. Finally, peace returned within.

Ignoring my neurotic guilt slowly began to become a habit. Every time I felt false guilt thereafter, I just boycotted it. And that has remained a habit with me to this present day. When it comes to neurotic guilt, just ignore it. It doesn't deserve a lot of rational attention. It won't listen anyway.

Keeping a clear conscience is vital to healthy thinking. It provides peace of mind and a positive outlook. Furthermore, If we don't settle the score with our conscience, we will be more likely to struggle with the next step: *Don't punish yourself.*

CHAPTER 8

Habit #4: Don't Punish Yourself

I am your God ... I see all of your actions. And I love you
because you are beautiful, made in my own image ...
Do not judge yourself. Do not condemn yourself. Do not
reject yourself ... Come, come, let me wipe your tears, and
let my mouth say ... I love you, I love you, I love you.
Henri Nouwen
The Road to Daybreak

The injunction "Don't punish yourself" naturally follows the previous two habits we have discussed. Both the refusal to allow ourselves to fail and the driving discomfort of a neurotic conscience can cause us to inflict punishment on ourselves. And self-punishment has got to be the most futile activity ever conceived.

Absurd as it is, however, most of us punish ourselves in big ways as well as in a host of subtle little ways. Even though we derive no benefit whatsoever from the pain we inflict, we continue to do it anyway. I suspect that, in the process, we also grieve the heart of God, who has offered us His forgiveness for the very sins, mistakes, and failures we're torturing ourselves about.

Julienne could have told you a lot about self-punishment. She was a tiny sparrow of a girl, which was why her anorexia looked particularly disfiguring. I first saw her as a patient when she was barely sixteen. Julienne was shy and seldom smiled, and hers was one of the first cases of anorexia I ever treated.

Anorexia nervosa was not a common disorder in the early days of clinical psychology. In fact, during my study years, only one case had shown up in our psychiatric hospital, and it caused quite a stir. Once the news got around that a case of anorexia had been admitted, the conference room was crowded with doctors, psychiatrists, psychologists, and nurses, anxious to observe a real live case. That's how rare it was thirty years ago. Today the condition is quite common, although not as complicated as the rarer and more serious form that presented itself in those early days.

There are many reasons why people, especially young girls from affluent, educated, success–driven homes, turn to starvation. Many just want to be thin because they fear fatness. Their families are usually stable but appearance–oriented, and looks may be a bit too important. While a few will eventually starve themselves to death, this is not where most anorexics are. Generally, they pass as very thin people, just teetering on the edge of skinniness.

Julienne's case, however, was more extreme. She clearly had a form of anorexia that was related to self–punishment. She seemed determined to starve herself out of existence. It had nothing to do with attracting boys or a fear of being fat. She had become convinced that she was an evil person and needed to be punished. Her anorexia nervosa was a symptom of a conscience gone bad.

Early Beginning of Self-Punishment

Julienne's first awareness of self-punishment took place at around twelve years of age when she began to pinch herself if she did something wrong. Later, she started pricking herself with a pin. Finally she learned how to starve herself, and starvation seemed to work better as a punishment than direct pain.

What started Julienne on this pursuit of self-punishment? One can never be absolutely sure about the causes. But for starters, her parents were deeply religious in a pathetically unhealthy way. They were extremely legalistic.

Religion (and I call it this rather than Christianity, though these parents thought they were devout Christians) was their life. I think one could call them Pharisaic believers. Legalism kept them feeling safe, which is what it usually does—with lots of rules, we never have to think or take any chances. As a result, religious people of this type become rigid and ruthless in their condemnation of everything that does not fit their rules for living.

This was Julienne's world. And, unfortunately, the effect it had on her was catastrophic, more than on any of her younger brothers. From an early age she felt "wicked." She desperately wanted to be good like her parents but just couldn't "feel good." They had many rules about what was right or wrong, and whether or not she violated any of them, she could never quite meet their standards of perfection.

To make matters worse, her parents would make up a rule *after* a supposed violation had occurred, then they would use it to condemn her. After school one day, her mother noticed that Julienne had walked home with a few classmates, new friends she had just made. Her mother instantly made up a rule that Julienne was to walk home alone because her parents had not "passed" her new friends as suitable companions. Then she scolded Julienne for having broken the rule she had just made up.

When the girl heard the message, it sounded something like this: "You should have known that we wouldn't condone your behavior, so you are a wicked person for not knowing better." We call these situations "double binds"—you can't win whatever you do or don't do, know or don't know. The guilt trips Julienne's parents laid on her lasted for weeks and weeks.

External Punishment Becomes Internalized

It wasn't just the unpredictability or strictness of the rules that was damaging to Julienne. I've encountered a lot of strict parenting, and it does not, of itself, cause permanent damage. It may set up a temporary period of rebellion, but this soon passes. What really did the damage to Julienne was the punishment inflicted by her parents, which was extremely subtle. Never did they physically chastise her. Nor did they display any anger. The fact that they hardly ever raised their voices added to their daughter's confusion, as well as their own. To this day, Julienne's parents cannot see what they might have done to cause their daughter such unhappiness.

In actuality, their idea of punishment was highly destructive. Instead of punishing her themselves by sending her to her room or removing some privilege, they laid the responsibility for this punishment on Julienne. "Well, what do you think we should do? We don't want to punish you. You've got to learn to take responsibility for yourself. So what should the consequence be for this bad behavior?"

Now don't misunderstand me. There is a lot of value in teaching children to take responsibility for their own actions. On several occasions as a father, I asked one of my daughters to reflect on what would be the appropriate discipline for some misbehavior. Such an approach is very appropriate for, say, an older adolescent whose conscience is already cast in stone and who needs to be challenged to think about the consequences of bad behavior.

It makes sense to say, "So, son, I let you take the family car and you said you would be home before midnight. But it was two o'clock before you came in. What do you think would be an appropriate consequence?" Hopefully he will suggest being grounded for a zillion years or at least for a couple of nights. This approach helps adolescents think about what it means to be responsible people. Besides, if the consequence is defined by the child, he or she can hardly object.

But such an approach is not helpful in dealing with a young child in the formative stage for moral development. And it is even more inappropriate when administered by rigid parents. Nevertheless, to Julienne's parents, it sounded quite reasonable and rational. They were exonerating themselves for any damage their punishment might cause by handing the instrument of punishment to her and saying, "Now you do whatever you think is appropriate."

The girl could never figure out exactly what it was they wanted, so she would just break down sobbing and run to her room. The parents would then leave her there, believing that self-rejection and humiliation was the best punishment of all. Never once did they ever offer her forgiveness. Never once did they show her a way to win back their approval.

Sometimes their message was, "So, what do you think God wants you to do to teach you to be a better girl?" Once they began to invoke God as part of the displeasure, they sealed Julienne's fate. Parents who think they can call on God to help them punish their children are contemptible. Excuse my strong language here, but I have just seen too much damage to use gentler words.

From her earliest years, then, Julienne was taught to internalize her own punishment. To some extent we all do this. We apply the strategies our parents have used to teach us right behavior—this is how the process of socialization works. But in Julienne's case it was carried to the extreme. "We will leave it to you, dear. If you think you should go to bed early because you missed the mark, then that's what you should do." Or . . . "It's not up to us to punish you. If you've been naughty then you must do what you think is right." To make matters worse, if what she offered to do (such as going to bed without any supper) was not acceptable, her parents would engage a second round of self-punishment.

Gradually, Julienne became a master at making herself unhappy whenever she felt guilt. She began to deprive herself of food, friends, and fun on a regular basis. And her parents never once intervened. They thought it was all very healthy, at least for a while. Then, at age twelve, matters got worse.

Julienne had just begun to feel sexual urges, and her parents had made it very clear that the most wicked thing a young girl could do was to experience any sexual feelings. They frequently paraded stories about "hussies" and "loose girls" who had become pregnant and were doomed to hell. Julienne had become quite phobic over sexual scenes on TV or school friends mentioning the topic. Sex began to take on a terrible connotation. One day while riding her bicycle home from school she accidentally began to rub herself against the seat. Instantly she felt aroused and almost fell off the bicycle. She pushed the bicycle home. Never again did she ride it.

She become obsessed with the fear that these sexual feelings proved that she was an evil person. She had felt sexual pleasure. There was only one thing to do. She stepped up her self-starvation. Depriving herself of food was always an effective punishment since she found pleasure in eating, and wicked people don't deserve any pleasure. In fact they don't even deserve to live.

Healing from Self-Punishment

My purpose in detailing Julienne's story is to illustrate how damaging self-punishment can be, and how subtle its origins are. We may not all suffer to the same extent as Julienne, but the dynamics of her case are common to all forms of self-punishment. To a lesser degree, I can see all of Julienne's distorted thinking in myself and certainly in many of my clients. At times, most of us have the habit of punishing ourselves whenever we do not live up to some internalized set of expectations.

The treatment of complicated anorexia is not easy. Weight gain alone will not solve the underlying problem. It involves two distinct tasks: normal nutrition and the underlying psychological conditions. Usually the whole family needs to be involved in treatment. I will spare you the details of Julienne's journey back to wholeness, but suffice it to say that her parents had to do more changing than she. The ingrained tendency to punish herself was to be Julienne's greatest battle, a battle I believe continues today, many years later.

Julienne's story illustrates that the basic ingredients are the same for all forms of self-punishment, whether it be physical, emotional, or even spiritual. There are myriad ways in which we punish ourselves. These include turning our anger inward, robbing ourselves of pleasure, acting out self-defeating behaviors, and failing to accomplish even the simplest of personal objectives. And it's all to no avail. Common as it is, self-punishment has absolutely no benefits whatsoever.

How can we break patterns of self-punishment that have been established over many years? As with many bad habits, we can best change them by forming a counterhabit. In other words, we make it a habit to do something different from the bad habit we want to break. Let me illustrate with two examples.

One Saturday morning I was standing in line at the supermarket, and I noticed a mother and her six-year-old son standing in front of me. They were Asian and obviously well-to-do. Suddenly I heard her scold the boy: "Don't do that! Keep your hands by your sides!"

At first I thought she was admonishing him for trying to sneak a bar of candy or something. She then turned to apologize to me for fear that her sudden outburst had startled me. "He keeps pulling out his hair," she explained, "and I'm trying to get him to stop it." I looked at the boy's head and saw evidence of the mother's concern. For a radius of three inches or so around his right ear he had indeed pulled out all his hair—I mean every hair. The area was naked and very noticeable because his hair was so black.

As I watched, the mother turned away, and the boy's hand went up to his head to feel for a strand. A quick tug and the halo on his hairless side grew a little larger.

I have seen this problem before in young children. It is often associated with high anxiety and a demanding atmosphere in the home. The mother shook her head in embarrassment and said, "Any suggestions?" Normally, I don't play psychologist outside the consulting room, but I couldn't ignore her plea for some guidance. I asked her whether her son had a tendency to be hard on himself.

"Yes," she replied, excited at the prospect that someone might understand what was happening to her boy. "That's exactly what he's like. I think he wants to punish himself for not being the best."

She said it, not I, and she was right on target. I encouraged her to think along these lines and to find ways she could reassure him for being who he is. I told her where she could get some professional help, but in the meantime I suggested that she buy a Gameboy or another of those little portable electronic games that children enjoy. I explained that until she could get to the bottom of her son's anxiety problem (because that's what it was) he needed to keep his hands busy doing something else that would compete with his hair pulling. She immediately understood the age-old principle: Idle hands are the devil's workshop.

"And one other thing," I called to her as she was about to leave the store. "Give him lots of love."

Here's another example. One of my patients says she has a tendency to find fault with the way other women dress. Whenever she goes anywhere, to church, to a party, to work, anywhere, she becomes critically preoccupied with the clothes other women are wearing. The habit drives her crazy. "I can't ever just meet people and like them for who they are. I judge them by their clothes, even though I realize it is ridiculous. After all, we all have different tastes, so why don't I just leave them be?"

I advised her to form a counterhabit. I explained that if she substituted a habit that was the exact opposite and practiced it regularly, she would eventually stop the bad one. We agreed that a good counterhabit would be to praise people for their clothes, no matter what they were wearing. This wasn't being dishonest since she agreed that different people have different tastes. Her criticism wasn't based on her own impeccable sense of style. In fact, it was the very opposite. She was honest enough to admit to the real problem—she didn't trust her own taste.

Every time this woman caught herself being critical, she quickly changed to the complimentary mode. She forced herself to say something nice, and when she did, she noticed that the other person's clothes actually looked better. It changed her perception dramatically. And once being complimentary became a good habit, her old bad habit faded away.

How can you apply this principle? Every time you catch yourself indulging in some self–punishment, switch to praising yourself. By doing so, giving positive encouragement becomes the healthier habit. You can't praise yourself and punish yourself at the same time.

We may never fully understand why we do it nor be totally free of wanting to punish ourselves. But we can choose not to do it. Here, as with so many psychological problems, right behavior eventually changes our feelings. And right behavior begins in the head. We have to get our thinking straight.

Recognizing Self-Punishment

I will leave to you the task of identifying why you punish yourself. Careful reflection will help you see patterns from your past that contribute to your self–punishment tendencies. Often, we cannot pinpoint any specific reason, which is why trying to discover the origin of a problem is not always a profitable pursuit. Some people are just born with sensitive genes.

Still, you may find it helpful to try and uncover the origin of the habit. Perhaps you can remember back to the second or third year of life and identify instances where you felt responsible for everything and felt bad because of it. Maybe you have foregone pleasure or allowed yourself to suffer because you felt badly about something or other. Gradually, feeling bad has become a way of life for you, and by now you may not know how to feel good about anything.

If this is the case, a good counterhabit is to deliberately seek out ways in which you can feel good about yourself. Do some charity work. Give sacrificially to a good cause in either time or money. Help someone in real need. And then allow yourself to feel good about it.

Self-Blame

Self-punishment sometimes takes one particular form, that of self-blame, and that subject deserves some special attention. One of the benefits of being human and having brains that can think is that our mind provides us with a mirror for self-reflection. God has given us the capacity to evaluate our actions. Animals don't have this benefit. They exist, and they follow their instincts. Whatever their capacity for thinking is, it falls far below ours.

Self-reflection is not always beneficial. Like those distorted mirrors you see in sideshows or at a fair, what you see isn't always what you are. You may look fat when you are thin, short when you are tall, and crooked when you are straight. It's all in the mirror. We often tend to be too critical, even harsh, with ourselves and what we see in the mirror of our self-reflection.

In fact, we have taken this wonderful gift of self-reflection and turned it into a monstrosity. God intended it to be the means of honest information about ourselves for growth and healing. But we have turned it into an instrument of punishment.

The psalmist invokes God's help in self-reflection with the prayer:

> *Search me, O God, and know my heart:*
> *Try me and know my thoughts:*
> *And see if there be any wicked way in me,*
> *and lead me in the way everlasting.*
> Ps. 139:23–24

In saying this, the ancient poet is opening himself to the profoundest measure of inner healing that a human is capable of experiencing. His is not a prayer for more information about how terrible he is in order to indulge in further self-blame. Instead, it is a prayer that leads him directly to the heart of God. It is the most authentic expression of what God intends for self-reflection, motivating us to know ourselves deeply and therefore to reach out for God, not for the cat-o'-nine-tails.

Healthy self-reflection is an act of openness to full discovery, a beckoning to expose our deepest secrets to the all-knowing Light of God's Spirit. The outcome is supposed to be our growth in wholeness.

So how has this gift of self-reflection become distorted? Instead of leaving the task of condemnation to God, we have taken it over ourselves. Of course God wants us to become aware of our weaknesses, not so we can punish ourselves for them, but so we can grow, with His help, into healthier creatures. That is why we have a conscience. Our awareness of sin causes us to repent and receive the forgiveness He has provided for us in Christ. Instead, we take over God's prerogative and do our own punishing.

The result? A subtle but profound form of mental affliction—the need to inflict pain or suffering on ourselves through self-blame, and thus to appease a deranged conscience. I realize I am using strong language here, but it shows how passionately I feel about this matter. People do more harm to themselves by self-inflicted vengeance than Satan could even begin to do. And by so doing, they usurp the work of God. He has offered us a better way. Why do we turn our backs on it?

A word of caution: Some people, as soon as they become aware that they judge and condemn themselves, begin to judge and condemn themselves for judging and condemning themselves! We sure are strange creatures, aren't we?

As we further explore bad habits and highlight their healthy counterparts, I trust we will see more and more what a wonderfully healing gospel God has given us. If we fail to become whole in mind and spirit, it is not because the Gospel is insufficient for our needs. It is because our grasp of the Gospel is so deficient.

CHAPTER 9

HABIT #5: VALUE LIFE'S LITTLE BLESSINGS

May we never let the things we can't have,
or don't have, or shouldn't have, spoil our enjoy-
ment of the things we do have and can have.
Richard L. Evans

In *The Guinness Book of Records* there is an entry that describes "The Greatest Miser." The person referred to is Hetty Green, a financier and New York Stock Exchange member whose desire for wealth utterly consumed her. Hetty was considered the richest woman of her day, and she was held in great awe. After inheriting a whaling and trade fortune, she invested and saved as much of it as she could. She maintained a bank balance of around $31 million, and when she died left an estate of almost $100 million.

Hetty neither spent her money nor enjoyed it. Her miserly lifestyle included living on cold oatmeal and existing in a frigid house because she was unwilling to spend money on heating. Her son had to have a leg amputated because she refused to pay for the operation that could have saved it.

To top it all off, Hetty Green was one of the meanest and unhappiest people who ever lived. If *The Guinness Book of Records* had a category for contemptible and despicable folks, she would have been listed there as well. Miser Hetty died in 1916 from a convulsion prompted by an argument over the virtues of skim milk!

The Best Things in Life

Hetty Green's story reminds us that the best things in life are free. It doesn't take money, at least not a lot of it, to make one happy. If history teaches us anything, it is that money usually has the opposite effect. Great wealth often breeds great unhappiness.

J. Paul Getty was another extremely successful and wealthy man whose fortune exceeded $1 billion. He lived most of his life in hotel rooms. A newspaper reporter once asked Getty, "Describe what money can't buy," and he answered: "I don't think it can buy health, and I don't think it can buy a good time. Some of the best times I have ever had didn't cost any money."

Of course, we're always a little skeptical (and perhaps a little envious) when we hear very wealthy people say that money can't buy health or happiness. Try telling that to a homeless person or to someone in abject poverty. Try telling it to hungry children in Somalia or to refugees in Bosnia. An excess of money may not make you any happier, but everyone has a need for a minimal amount of money, or its equivalent, just to survive in the modern world. What very wealthy people really mean when they say that "money isn't everything" is that, beyond a certain point, you don't become any happier by possessing more money.

Happiness Is in the Little Things

My point here is that we will never ever be really contented, or happy, or fulfilled unless we know how to appreciate the "little" things of life. There is a level beyond which no amount of prosperity will bring any more happiness. And I want to suggest that this level is a lot lower than most of us assume. We need to make a habit of enjoying that which costs nothing, or very little, or else we will never be able to enjoy whatever level of prosperity God allows us to have.

What gets in the way of our appreciating the little things? Money, of course. The problem is not about having too much money. That's one thing. But the real concern with ordinary folks like us, who only have enough to get by on, is that we erroneously believe that having more money will make life rosier. Because of this belief, we neglect the enjoyment that little things can bring. If we are not careful, this neglect can easily usurp our happiness.

J. Paul Getty was right after all. "Some of the best times . . . didn't cost any money." Not only did they not cost any money, but I suggest that no amount of money could have bought them. What price can one put on watching a beautiful sunset with someone you love? Enjoying a moment of closeness with grand-children? Watching the birth of your child? Creating something beautiful with your own hands?

This doesn't mean we are not entitled to reasonable living costs. What it does mean is that once we have provided the abso-lute basics of life, like a roof over our heads and food on our tables, we'd better start looking for real happiness in the little, free things of life. Shape this habit as strongly as you possibly can, because if you don't, you may end up a bit like Hetty Green: disappointed and disillusioned!

The Roots of Discontentment

An Associated Press release was headlined, "Americans Said Healthy but Feel Lousy." The report went on to say that Americans have never been healthier, but that they feel worse than ever before—a phenomenon that has become known in medical circles as "the paradox of health." The paradox of health means that even when you have every reason to feel healthy, you don't. This para-dox not only applies to our physical health but also to the health of our psyches.

I believe there is also a "paradox of contentment" operating in our culture. We have every reason to feel happy and contented because we are healthier and wealthier than anyone in history. We are better off than any person of similar circumstances elsewhere in the world. Nonetheless, we feel discontented. Dissatisfaction seems to have become the American way.

What lies behind this paradox of contentment? Several things. For one, I think that even though we are healthier and live longer (in 1900 life expectancy was forty–seven; now it is seventy–five years) our increased longevity has given us more time to experience unhappiness. If life is basically meaningless for someone, the longer that person lives, the more protracted is his or her misery.

Industry reports twice as many episodes of work–interfering illness per capita in the 1980s as it did in the 1920s. How can this be true when in the 1920s, there were no antibiotics to help overcome illnesses? It isn't really illness that keeps some people away from work. There are individuals who simply don't want to work. They find no fulfillment in their occupations, so they call in sick. People didn't do this in the '20s.

There is another reason for the paradox of contentment. Even though we have bigger and better gadgets, faster cars, more elaborate toys, and more colorful entertainment than our forebears, it has only fed our discontent. The glut of "big" and exciting things to enjoy has desensitized us to the real and abiding pleasure that simpler things provided. We have become addicted to excitement and have to keep upping the ante to feel stimulated, which amounts to a classic addiction spiral.

I did not see this discontentment in my grandparents nor in the world they lived in. My grandfather retired at fifty–five, just as World War II was beginning. He had only a small pension and little savings to live on. He and my grandmother grew all their food on the small piece of land abutting their home, and to my young eyes they lived royally. They produced the most delicious tomatoes, and their home–dried fruit tasted better than the most expensive candy. For entertainment, they listened to a small short-wave radio each evening.

Their life was simplicity itself, and yet my brother and I valued our times with them above everything else. We walked everywhere because gas was scarce, fished and swam freely in the river nearby, and sat under the stars pumping water into the storage tank with a hand pump every evening. It was bliss, unmitigated joy.

I regret sometimes that my lifestyle isn't that simple and uncomplicated. My children and grandchildren have lost out because their world is more sophisticated and costly. We have become so accustomed to expensive things that we have forgotten just how much real pleasure can be had for nothing.

And, oddly enough, the pleasure of little things is not addicting. Isn't that interesting?

Crisis—A Real Eye-Opener

A minister friend had a heart attack a few years ago. He is a charming and charismatic person as well as being high–pressured and dynamic. He can outpreach anyone I know, although I'm not sure whether that is a good thing or bad.

Heart disease, of the sort caused by high–adrenaline excitement, knocked him flat one day. It came out of the blue. He always thought he was invincible and indestructible, and in some ways he was. But he was not attending to the pressures and demands of his busy life and stress disease was working its destruction silently in the background. In many respects, he had become unbalanced. He thought that only the "big" things mattered, like preaching to large crowds and achieving great goals. He neglected the little things, like taking breaks, enjoying a vacation, or just spending time relaxing and smelling the flowers.

It took this preacher's heart attack to really shake up his priorities. Lying in the hospital after a quadruple bypass, he rediscovered God. He also discovered a great theological truth: God is first interested in our worship and only then in our service. He had put the cart before the horse. The pursuit of "big" issues of his ministry, not the pursuit of God (and there is a difference), was what had nearly killed him.

During his postsurgical recovery, my friend changed some of his priorities. He began to get up early in the morning and go into his backyard. There he would sit quietly under a tree, enjoying the fragrance of the flowers, watching the birds, basking in the warm sun. During one of these rest times he caught sight of a family of blue jays who had nested in a nearby tree. He didn't know that birds lived in his yard, because he had never seen nor heard them.

Before long, he found himself eagerly looking forward to getting home from work so he could check up on the blue jays. It thrilled him to observe the cycle of their lives, their comings and goings, their nest-building, feeding babies, fighting over morsels of food, and enjoying the simple life God had given to them. Somehow, their existence seemed to be much nearer to the heart of God than this preacher's crazy, activity-driven existence. The words of Jesus in the Sermon on the Mount became very precious to him:

> Take no thought for your life, what ye shall eat,
> or what ye shall drink . . . Behold the fowls of the air:
> for they sow not, neither do they reap, nor gather into barns;
> yet your heavenly Father feedeth them.
>
> Matt. 6:25–26

A great peace came over my friend every time he sat in his garden watching those beautifully colored birds. It began to change his life for the better. The power of little things is able to work miracles.

When Did We Lose Our Innocence?

Recently as I reviewed a major textbook on mental disorders in preparation for a class I was to teach, I came across the following words: "Children typically seem to feel happy, whereas grownups do not." These profound words were written by a very prestigious professor of psychopathology. They got my attention.

Essentially, he was saying that we all start life happy, but somewhere along the way to adulthood we lose that happiness. I know this has been true for me, and I strongly suspect it is true for you, too. But what goes wrong? Where do we lose the innocence and simplicity that begets happiness?

The textbook goes on to explain that children are more spontaneous in their social behavior than adults and that their natural mood is more elevated and joyful. To put it simply, children know how to enjoy themselves. Growing up inoculates us against being playful, or more accurately, causes us to turn to more elaborate enjoyments to make ourselves happy. And the loss of this simplicity means the loss of happiness. Sad, isn't it?

Children are happier because they know how to enjoy the little things of life—a visit to the park, a stopover with grandparents, walking barefoot in a rain puddle, watching a steam engine, a ride in a boat, a first, daring dive into a public swimming pool, and even the smell of blossoms at the beginning of spring. I mention these specific sources of pleasure because they are the ones I remember best from my own childhood. They are on my long list of simple, and mostly free little things, the memory of which can still produce profound pleasure within me.

Perhaps I am fortunate in having enjoyed numerous little pleasures while growing up during World War II when resources were applied to the war effort. We had to recycle everything and could buy very few new things. There were no toy factories, so a child could not buy a kite, toy gun, bicycle, or even chewing gum, no matter how much money he or she had. As a result, we had to create our own toys just as children in bygone ages once did.

As I reflect back on how we did this, I honestly think we derived greater pleasure from our crude, self-fabricated playthings than my children and grandchildren have derived from their factory-made equivalents. We made cars out of tomato-box wood, using whatever implements we could lay our hands on to cut wheels, drill holes, and join wood. We shaped toy soldiers out of sunbaked clay, and painted them with mud mixed with beet-root juice. We invented gadgets woven from bottle tops, cotton reels, and string. We collected foil and made huge balls out of it. We were forced to be creative and inventive by using our imagination to make up for the lack of realism. And I believe we were the better for it. I am convinced that little things—the simple doohickeys and distractions of life—provide us with a lot more pleasure than big, complicated, and expensive items we yearn to buy.

Is it any wonder that when we grow wealthier we also become more miserable? If we do not notice birds, smell roses, or watch sunsets, how can we ever expect to find any satisfaction in our possessions?

The Scent of Days Gone By

To illustrate these little pleasures, let me tell you about one I discovered for myself. Many springs ago, I was taking a nighttime walk, and I happened to stroll past a house in a nearby neighborhood. I had never been on this street before. Suddenly I caught the whiff of a flowering shrub. Instantly a flood of early childhood memories overwhelmed me—the smell was identical to that of a shrub a neighbor had when I was a child. I had not smelled that aroma since I was six or seven years old, but the memory of it was deeply locked in my mind. Catching its scent again brought forth all sorts of happy thoughts about my childhood. I stopped, turned, and lingered near that home for quite a while, experiencing enormous pleasure as I savored the fragrance.

I had started out my walk that evening feeling very angry. It had been a hard day. Things hadn't gone well, and I was feeling that everyone was against me. I was oozing self-pity. But as I lingered around that bush, which filled the air all around with its aroma, my tension subsided. How could life be so bad when there were scents like this to be enjoyed and wonderful memories to be relived? I found the courage to break off a blossom–covered twig and carried it home with me, holding it close to my nostrils from time to time just to refresh my memory. Smell may be a little thing, but it can make a person feel sane again.

The Stream of Little Pleasures

We are constantly gifted with a stream of little things that can help to restore our mental and emotional balance and provide us with a rich resource for happiness. All we need to do is learn how to recognize and appreciate them, to make a habit of seeking them out and enjoying them.

Along with the pleasures of nature, we can enjoy the creativity of others through music, poetry, art, and books. And let us not forget the precious gifts of Scripture and prayer—ours for the receiving.

We are all different. What excites me may bore you to death. How can you discover what fits the category of delightful little things for you? Let me suggest an exercise that can help you develop a list of little things you can really enjoy.

Find yourself a small notebook or carry a few index cards with you. As you go through each day, pay careful attention to the little blessings you experience. Perhaps a stranger greeted you on the bus. Your walk through the park took you past a few ducks on a pond. You completed the crossword puzzle in the newspaper. Make a note of anything and everything, no matter how small or seemingly insignificant, that gave you even the slight- est joy. Write it down right then and there, because you will quickly forget it as the larger issues of life rush in on you.

Before going to sleep at bedtime, take a few minutes to reflect on your day. Ask yourself what it was that gave you the greatest pleasure during the day and make a note of it. Like me, you probably have a time of the day or an activity that helps you to be reflective. For me it is while taking a bath. For you, it may be during some other quiet activity.

While you're relaxing, keep your notebook close at hand and try to recall happy times from your past. Include the things that made you happy or drew you closer to God. Ask God to remind you of them, and jot them down.

After a while you will begin to identify several little things you can do, see, or experience that give you deep pleasure. Make a summary of these on a single card and keep this card in a place where you can review it. Then, when you need some cheer or an emotional lift, indulge yourself in one of these little blessings.

William James, a Christian who was one of the early pioneers of what we refer to as scientific psychology, said that "the greatest discovery of my generation is that a human being can alter his life by altering his attitudes of mind." Changing your attitude to value life's little blessings can bring great changes to your tem- perament and outlook. It works for me, and I believe it will do the same for you.

CHAPTER 10

HABIT #6: ACCENTUATE THE POSITIVE

There is very little difference in people.
But that little difference makes a big difference.
The little difference is attitude.
The big difference is whether it is positive or negative.
W. Clement Stone

I have a three-year-old granddaughter named Caitlan. She's a real cutie pie and voguishly smart. Lately she's discovered the word "attitude," and she even seems to have some sense of what it means. Whenever her older sister or one of her cousins frustrates her or seems to be out of sorts, she marches up to the guilty party, puts on her most grown-up voice, and asks, hands on hips, "Why you got a attitude?" The translation is simple: "You are bugging me. Why do you persist in maintaining such a negative attitude? Try being a little more positive, okay?"

I wish I could describe the look on her little face when she confronts the offender. It's a cross between being perplexed and forecasting some terrible catastrophe. It's the cutest look you can imagine.

Caitlan's amusing reference to "having a attitude" whenever she sees someone being ornery has helped to raise our family's consciousness about just how important one's attitude really is. Our first reaction, of course, was to break out in hilarious laughter. But now we all find ourselves on guard against combative or quarrelsome behavior. The last thing anyone wants is to be on the receiving end of one of Caitlan's challenges!

Hugh Downs, the well-known TV broadcaster, recently stated, "A happy person is not a person in a certain set of circumstances but rather a person with a certain set of attitudes." It is the set of our attitudes that I want to focus on here. Going through life with the wrong set of attitudes will guarantee failure or misery or both. Creating a positive attitude is as important a habit as any I will be discussing here.

Attitude Infects Everything

At a research center in Salisbury, England, technicians infect volunteers with one of the world's oldest afflictions, the common cold. The viruses that cause the common cold (called rhinoviruses, of which there are one hundred distinct varieties) are around us all the time. However, we only "catch cold" when certain conditions prevail. The question these researchers are exploring is why some people get sick while others don't, even when they are all together in the same chilly place. Ultimately they hope to find a cure for the cold, but in the meantime they are questioning why our different immune systems make some of us more susceptible to colds than others.

What has this got to do with Caitlan's "Why you got a attitude?" As the scientists perform blood tests to measure the immune system responses of their subjects, they also ask a lot of personal questions. They are exploring the attitudes of their subjects. They ask questions like: Are you happily married? Does your work cause you a lot of hassles? And, most important of all, are your attitudes positive or negative? Are you optimistic or pessimistic?

I find this an absolutely fascinating line of research. We have long known that attitude affects the immune system, which is why, even in the treatment of cancer, a lot of attention is given to ensuring the right state of mind. Attitudes affect the healing process. If you surrender to your illness, the immune system doesn't do as good a job of fighting as when you maintain a positive attitude. Since the mind holds sway over the body in numerous ways, these researchers are trying to connect different mind–sets with the body's resistance to viral diseases like the common cold.

To observe how the mind influences the body we need look no further than the effect that shame or embarrassment has on us. Whenever we feel shame, blood rushes to the face in a telltale blush. The reaction in our mind triggers a physical reaction that flushes certain parts of the skin. The reaction is automatic. Upsetting news also causes physical reactions, such as dizziness or nausea.

So what does a bad attitude do to the body? Researchers are finding that negative attitudes and emotional states affect the body's immune system in very profound ways, and the influence is destructive. What this means is that good attitudes produce greater health than bad attitudes. These researchers predict that their discoveries are going to play an important part in revolutionizing how doctors treat such disabling illnesses as breast cancer, migraine headaches, ulcers, insomnia, high blood pressure, and many other disorders.

A Matter of Positive Attitude

Have you noticed how chronic complainers get sick a lot? When I was growing up, one of our neighbors was a very nice woman. She was kind to the neighborhood children and didn't complain too much about our boyish pranks. She had the largest fruit orchard in the neighborhood, and a lot of ripe fruit would have fallen to the ground and gone to waste if we hadn't rescued the situation. We would occasionally scale her high wall in the dead of night and feast on figs, apricots, and peaches. And we reckoned we were actually doing her a favor, since she never complained to our parents.

That poor woman did complain about everything else, however. It was wartime, and a lot of fathers, brothers, and husbands were "up north" fighting in Northern Africa. My own father was one of them, and so was this lady's husband. How much this contributed to her unhappiness I don't know, but I clearly remember her as a very negative person who constantly complained.

She was also sick a lot. As I reflect back on her frequent illnesses, I can't help suspecting that there was a connection between her illnesses and her negativity. And now there is scientific evidence that connects the two.

The health impact of negative attitudes and thinking has been demonstrated by many studies, and I don't want to belabor this point here. However, one study is of special significance because it is what is called a "longitudinal study." It followed the same group of Harvard graduates over a very long period of time. In 1937, researchers got a group of Harvard students to complete an extensive questionnaire about their emotional and physical health. They then followed each subject over subsequent years. Many of those original Harvard graduates have now reached old age, and many have died.

The researchers' findings are extremely informative. It seems that those with the most negative attitudes at age twenty-five suffered the most serious illnesses in their forties, fifties, and sixties when compared with their more positive classmates. What does this mean? Some have tried to say that their proclivity toward illness made these people negative, not the other way around—a "which came first, the chicken or the egg?" type of question.

But the results are clear: It wasn't illness that soured these people and turned them into negative thinkers. Instead, their negativity soured their bodies. The information about their negative attitudes was gathered before there was any evidence of illness—at least twenty years before any of the subjects had experienced any illness. Negative attitudes were evident in the group that was more prone to illness long before any of them became ill. Furthermore, it was the pre-existing positive attitudes that protected those less prone to illness. There is no doubt about which is the chicken and which is the egg in this particular case.

But this is not new information. You don't have to go back very far in history to find a time when all we had to fight disease was our own immune systems. Attitude was even more important then. That's why James Allen, who lived around the turn of the century, wrote: "At the bidding of unlawful thoughts the body sinks rapidly into disease and decay; at the command of glad and beautiful thoughts it becomes clothed with youthfulness and beauty."

Health and disease are rooted in thought, and there is nothing magical about this relationship. It is not mind over matter as some would like to think. Thought can simply affect the immune system, the stress–response system, and a host of other physiological systems in profound ways. Sickly, fearful, and stressful thoughts will produce stress and a defensive response in the body. One of the penalties for this stress is that the body has to divert its actions away from disease protection to fighting the external threats it perceives. Healthy, uplifting, encouraging thoughts stimulate the immune system, lower stress, increase the natural tranquilizers in the brain, and make us healthier. Again, we are looking at a simple matter of cause and effect.

Is It Too Late to Change?

In light of such overwhelming scientific evidence linking negative attitudes to illness and emotional turmoil, the important question you are probably asking is this: Can the influence of years and years of negative thinking be reversed?

Well, I have good news and bad news. The good news is that we can reverse the damaging effects of negative thinking. If we couldn't, we'd all be in a lot of trouble because we all go through negative periods of life.

The bad news is that you can't afford to wait until you start getting sick and then decide to change. Once your immune system has deteriorated, it will take a long time to rejuvenate itself. Simply stated, the earlier in your life you change from being a negative thinker to a positive thinker, the greater your prospect of building a healthier body and mind and the more likely you are to undo the damaging effects of a glum disposition. Now is the time to begin.

Figuring prominently in the findings of recent research about how one can reverse the effects of negativity are three essential ingredients to better health. These are:

1. The importance of exercise

2. The body's need for relaxation

3. The development of positive attitudes

The first two are unquestionably important. The body needs to be well exercised, especially if we work in sedentary occupations. The body also needs time for relaxation when the adrenal system can be allowed to rejuvenate itself. Exercise and relaxation are the strongest and most effective antidotes we have to fight stress disease. You will find help in these two areas by consulting my book *The Hidden Link Between Adrenaline and Stress* (Word Publishing, 1995). In this context, however, I want to focus on the importance of the third ingredient, accentuating the positive, and making it an abiding habit.

Positive Thinking—Cliché or Clincher?

I'll be honest. There are times when I feel like strangling the next person who says to me, "Oh come on, think positively about what has happened." The idea of positive thinking has become so trite, such a cliché, that I almost feel it should be banished from normal conversation. Fortunately, there is a marked difference between genuine positive attitudes and positive thinking as it is popularly portrayed

Most people, when they use the expression "Think positively," really mean something like: "Let's just deny that such and such has happened. If we ignore it, it will go away. Just put on a happy face and forget all the terrible things that have happened to you." This does a great disservice to those who teach a genuine, forthright, and honest adoption of a positive mind-set. I will have more to say about the unpalatable variations of the positive thinking concept in the next chapter. For now, let us accept that there is a healthy and necessary way to think positively, and it is not a form of denial or a refusal to face life's realities.

Can you tell whether you have a positive outlook? Yes, you can. Take the following test. Answer each question as honestly as possible, rating yourself with:

> **3** if your answer is always,
> **2** if it is sometimes,
> **1** if it is occasionally
> **0** if never.

1. Do you thank a person who finds fault or criticizes you for whatever was truthful?

2. When a stranger stares at you do you think it is because he/she likes you?

3. When there is a sudden change of plans or an obstacle to your goal, do you see a hidden advantage in the change or obstacle?

4. Are you able to compliment others for their success?

5. Do you remember your past successes more than your failures?

6. Do you easily recover from setbacks?

7. By and large, does life seem good to you?

These seven questions are by no means exhaustive. They merely illustrate the sort of thoughts and reactions that go along with positive thinking.

How did you do? Your total score can be interpreted as follows:

16–21: Excellent. You are thoroughly positive in your outlook. I only hope you've been completely honest!

11–15: Good. You are sometimes a positive person and have a foundation on which to build.

8–10: Fair. Your outlook could certainly do with an overhaul.

Below 8: You are in trouble. You clearly need to work on your negative tendencies.

The Origin of Negative Thinking

I don't usually spend a lot of time discussing the origins of anything, and particularly not emotional or thinking problems. We cannot always, with certainty, explain the origin or place the blame on any specific cause for an emotional difficulty. And even if we could identify the source of a problem, chances are that it wouldn't make any difference in our behavior or feelings anyway.

Just knowing the why of things doesn't, by itself, modify anything. We still have to make up our minds to change.

However, when it comes to negative thinking, we may be able to derive some value in reviewing its origin, if only to emphasize that the solution lies entirely within ourselves. Contrary to popular opinion, we are not programmed at birth to be either positive or negative individuals. Our thinking patterns grow out of our early experiences. Patterns of thought are learned and then become automatic.

Because our thinking patterns are formed when we are still very young, we don't recognize what is happening at the time. Day after day, week after week, we receive messages or observe reactions in others that we begin to internalize in our minds. Suppose Mom gets a letter from someone. She doesn't want to open it because she's afraid it might contain bad news. We learn from her to expect bad news in letters.

Dad tries to fix the toaster. He opens it and can't find the problem, so he throws the toaster in the trash can and says, "They don't make things like they used to!" We learn that there is no point in trying to fix anything because everything is unfixable—Dad said so.

With practice, a negative mind-set becomes more and more automatic. Soon it defines who we are. And it will be with us to the grave unless we take steps to undo the automatic way negative thinking operates.

Changing Negative Thinking

It is not as difficult to change negative thinking as you might suspect. With a careful plan of attack and an objective approach, you will begin to see changes in a matter of days. There are three steps in the process:

1. Increasing awareness of your negative thoughts

2. Responding to these negative thoughts

3. Taking actions against them

I will briefly mention each of these here. However, in section three of this book you will find several exercises that apply these basic steps to problems, some of which go far beyond negative thinking.

Step 1: Increase awareness of your negative thoughts. Most negative thoughts lurk as vague, unfocused notions below our level of awareness. I won't call them unconscious because this word has too much baggage associated with it. Let's just say we're simply not aware when we think negative stuff. However, the fact that we are not aware of our negative thoughts doesn't reduce their power to pulverize our emotions and sabotage our successes. In fact, our unaware condition increases our thoughts' negative power.

Our first offensive technique against negative thoughts is to bring them into the open where we can see and hear them.

The enemy is half-beaten when you know where and what it is. Dealing with negative thought is like eradicating cockroaches. A few times in my life I've had to deal with them, usually when we've moved to a new home. A week or two after moving in, you turn a light on and see one scurrying away. That's all you need to know—one cockroach always means a horde. They breed profusely, like negative thoughts, and you don't want to be lulled into a false comfort by thinking there is only one of them. Before you can purge them from your abode, you've got to find them. So it is with negative thoughts.

A second technique is to use the instant-replay technique.

If you've ever watched football on TV you will know how to stage an instant replay. Whenever you catch yourself feeling low or angry, think back to whatever crossed your mind before your mood changed. Replay the thoughts, actions, and self-talk that preceded your changed mood.

Did you label yourself as worthless? Did you believe some action of yours was idiotic? Think of yourself as a TV sports producer and call for an instant replay, then write down the thoughts or actions that led up to the mood change. You'll quickly begin to uncover the ugly little distortions in your mind that would otherwise go undetected.

A third technique is to monitor your thoughts at regular intervals and count the number of negative thoughts as they occur.

Small counters are available for tallying everything from golf strokes to knitting stitches. Or, as you detect negative thinking, you may choose to remain low-tech and simply transfer coins from one pocket to another or from one side of your purse to the other. This helps to raise your awareness of when and where your negative thinking begins. Your goal here is simply to turn vague, diverse thoughts into conscious, concrete ones. Once you can see them, you can begin to kill them off.

Step 2: Respond to negative thoughts. Now you move from being an exterminator to being a hard-nosed prosecutor, the sort you see on *Court TV*. When you have identified a particular negative thought that is troubling you, put it in the witness chair and start cross-examining the culprit. Be as objective and honest as possible—no game playing, no excuses. Challenge the thought by asking, "What gives you the right to say that? Where's the evidence that everything is hopeless? How do you know that things won't get better?"

The purpose here is to challenge all negative thoughts and to convince yourself that they are not true. Even if some of them are true, this step will show you what remedial action you have to take to repair the situation.

It is very helpful for you to write down your challenges so that you can make use of them later, because you will find that many negative thoughts repeat themselves over and over again. This should cause you to push even harder as the prosecutor. "You said that yesterday, and I disproved it then. I am doing so again today."

You will also find that negative thoughts often contradict each other. That's what all lies do. Catch yourself in contradictions and hammer home every one just as you would if you were the prosecutor in a courtroom.

Step 3: Take action against negative thoughts. Let me change the analogy one more time. We've gone from being an exterminator to being a prosecutor, and now we move to being a coach. It's not enough simply to identify and challenge the rationality of negative thoughts; you've also got to take action against them.

That means coaching yourself to take the right action, no matter what your feelings.

Let's suppose that you repeatedly tell yourself that you can't do something such as teach a Sunday school class or speak publicly. What's your reason? You think you are too stupid, small, big, old, female, male, uneducated, depressed, or anxious.

You know the thought is negative. You've counted it a trillion times in your head and had it in court for longer than any famous trial. Now you've got to take some action against it. What this usually means is going out and doing the very thing you fear or believe you can't do. I mean it. Take action! Pray for God to help you and launch out.

There are only two possible outcomes from any action you decide to take, and either way you win. Either you will find you can do what you thought you couldn't or that you can't. If you can, go on doing it. If you can't, give it up and try something else. You now have proof that God intends you for something better, so move on. Most times, however, people discover that they really can do what they most fear.

Accentuating the Positive

The elimination of negative patterns of thinking will not automatically guarantee the emergence of positive patterns. The absence of the one will not necessarily create the other. One can go from being negative to having no opinions whatsoever, just being apathetic or neutral. A positive attitude is more than this. It is a deliberate set of carefully chosen attitudes that can become as automatic as negative ones.

An apt analogy is one we've used before—that of a magnificent garden. A positive attitude is more than the absence of weeds, it is the presence of beautiful flowers and well-placed shrubbery. It requires design and intentional cultivation. So, once you've taken the time to remove the weeds of negativity, you need to begin planting the flowers of buoyant and constructive thought. In the spirit of the old song, we must learn to "accentuate the positive," not just eliminate the negative.

The most effective technique yet devised for this is the use of positive self-affirmations. Some Christians feel uncomfortable doing this. If so, then let Christ affirm you. Take some prayer time and be open to listening to what God would say to you. It's a lot more loving and tender than what you say to yourself!

Self-affirmations must be truthful. I say this because there is an instinctive resistance in some religious circles, especially more conservative Christian circles of the sort I affiliate with, to any self-affirming notions. The self, they say, cannot be trusted. Better that we don't affirm it. I don't disagree with these criticisms altogether. In fact, I wrote about this problem in one of my books because I was concerned about how easily we take self-affirmations too far. (See *Me, Myself and I*, Servant Publications.)

But here's another situation where we've thrown the baby out with the bathwater. We have a self, and if this self has been regenerated or born again, then it is a self that should be fully yielded to God's control. I don't believe God takes pleasure in our negative or bad thinking. In fact, I know He doesn't. Through Paul He encouraged us to think only about good things. (See Phil. 4:8.) Positive self-affirmations are in this genre if they are honest. It is the dishonest and exaggerated self-affirmations that the critics remind us to avoid, and rightly so.

Here, then, are six Christ-based, positive self-affirmations. Use them to develop a set of self-statements you can trust. God will bless them to your heart and mind if you are honest. Remind yourself of them in moments of disappointment and allow God to draw you to Him with the gentle prompting of His Spirit. Self-affirmations that follow these rules are expressions of God's deepest concern and love for you.

Affirmation #1: God loves me more than I can ever imagine, and I can never travel beyond the reach of this great love (Rom. 8:39).

Affirmation #2: No matter what my sin, God forgives me if I repent, confess and return to Him (1 John 1:9 and Ps. 103:10–12).

Affirmation #3: There is nothing I can do that will cause God to turn away from me (Heb. 13:5).

Affirmation #4: Whatever I attempt to do, if it is God's will for me He will give me the strength and wisdom I need to accomplish the task (Phil. 4:13).

Affirmation #5: If I seem to fail because circumstances are against me, God will always give me another opportunity if I return to the starting point (Ps. 37:24).

Affirmation #6: God never wants me to give up. Never, never, never, never (Josh. 1:5, 7, 9).

Affirmation #7: Hating myself doesn't make God love me more; it just makes it harder for me to see His love (Ps. 103:10–12).

Add your own affirmations. Make them short, clear, unambiguous, and specific. Avoid negative terms like *stop*, *not*, or *don't*. Repeat your affirmations often, and you will slowly see your negativity recede as positive and more truthful attitudes take its place. You will then be well on the way to accentuating the positive, which is a key habit of a healthy mind.

CHAPTER 11

HABIT #7:
BE THE RIGHT SORT OF OPTIMIST

For myself I am an optimist—it does not
seem to be much use being anything else.
Sir Winston Churchill

A n optimist thinks an unmatched sock is an extra one. An
optimist sees the doughnut, a pessimist, the hole.

Michel De Saint-Pierre once wrote, "An optimist may see a
light where there is none, but why must the pessimist always run
to blow it out?"

Why do we joke about optimists and pessimists? Because we
see ourselves in both of them. There is no such thing as a pure
optimist or pessimist; even though one or the other perspective
may dominate, we are all a mixture of each. With that in mind, it
is fair to ask yourself: Are you fundamentally an optimist or a
pessimist?

One year for my birthday, my daughter Sylvia sent me two
little statues from Germany that I now keep prominently displayed on my consulting–room desk. One is entitled "The Pessimist." As you can imagine, he has a pathetic, downcast look on
his face. The other is called "The Optimist." I wish I could describe
his expression, which is a cross between rapture and joviality. It
is the face of a man who has just been told by the dentist that he
doesn't need a root canal after all.

These little statues take a place of pride in my office. Every client gets a good chance to appreciate them, because they stare down at us as we try to solve life's mysteries. Each face has special appeal because it emphasizes a common stereotype of optimists and pessimists: One is happy and the other one is miserable.

Now you may be wondering why I am discussing optimism as a separate subject from a positive attitude. Are they not one and the same? For many people they are. If someone is positive in outlook, surely he or she is also optimistic. Interestingly, this is not true for everyone. A positive, realistic attitude is always healthy. But sometimes what appears to be optimism is merely a naive avoidance of reality. I am always suspicious of people who are overly optimistic. What world do they live in? Certainly not the one I inhabit.

If you wish to test whether too much optimism is a good thing ask yourself: Was Jesus an optimist? The very question seems a violation of the character of Jesus. Somehow it doesn't fit. He saw too much suffering and felt too much pain to be identified solely by such a label. On the other hand, He wasn't a pessimist either. His example alone indicates that there has got to be a balance constituting what a healthy attitude is all about.

I've never been able to make up my mind which I am. Whether I am an optimist or a pessimist seems to depend on the day of the week, the time of the day, the weather, world news, local news, and who I'm with. My mood seems to have direct control over my optimism and can turn it on or off at will, or so it seems.

I do know, however, that it pays to lean toward optimism as a habit, and that's what I want to emphasize here. There is a lot of good stuff associated with having a cheerful, hopeful outlook, as we will see. Meanwhile, in thirty years of psychological investigation and study I have not been able to find one good thing to say about pessimism. Battles have been lost, opportunities sacrificed, and ambitions extinguished by pessimistic perspectives.

Optimism Is a State Not a Trait

Right at the outset let me make one point clear: Optimism or pessimism are attitudes we choose rather than states that are thrust upon us. We learn them. Sure, there are people who are perpetually pessimistic. I know, because I have often met them. They have chosen to be the way they are, and they can change if they want to. Optimism replaces pessimism only when we decide to make it a habit of our minds. We can switch off the one and switch on the other.

Most of us have to struggle, at least occasionally, with feelings of pessimism when we feel gloomy and ill-fated. The pessimism doesn't last, but it passes through our lives. Our challenge, when gloom visits, is to tune into the optimistic way of thinking. The more we master the habit of optimistic thinking, the less pessimism will bother us.

Positive attitudes are always healthy, but optimism needs some safeguards, and the way to safeguard against unhealthy optimism is to always balance it with reality. Optimism without a solid reality check is called *denial*, and when we use denial excessively, our thinking is about as unhealthy as it can get.

Denial often masquerades as faith in our Christian subculture. When some Christians are faced with fearful situations, they simply jump behind some spiritual cliché and refuse to look reality in the face. And by the way, I'm talking about real fear. Imagined fear has no place in the believer's life, because it is the product of distorted thinking or out-of-control anxiety. But real fear must be faced. And optimism, cloaked in spiritual language, is still denial of that fear, no matter how good it feels.

Denial is a far cry from true faith. Faith always acknowledges the truth and is then able to turn for help to the coping resources that God provides for us. "Yes, this lump is a cancer. Two doctors have told me so. I will turn this over to God and trust that He will guide me in what I should do." This is faith.

Denial doesn't acknowledge the truth, it tries to avoid it. Denial says, "They can say what they like, I just won't accept that I have cancer. What do doctors know anyway? I'm just going to believe that it doesn't exist, and it will go away." You may be asking yourself, do Christians really think like this? Unfortunately, yes. They do it all the time.

The advantage that faith has over denial is that faith will seek the right solution. Denial does not face up to the truth and therefore does not seek timely remedies. Never confuse real faith with its wishy-washy counterfeit. Denial is deadly, and I mean this both literally and figuratively.

At the personal level, denial represses feelings. Those feelings remain submerged, nevertheless, and continue to work their destruction. In this sense, denial eventually brings us down, whereas honest faith builds us up. Denial is unhealthy; faith is healthy. Faith is our helper and healer because it puts us and keeps us in touch with God.

Beware of "Positive Illusions"

In psychological circles, researchers have recently begun to study the value of something called "positive illusions." This is a variation of optimism that is based on imagination. It is a way of using subtle deception to fool the mind into being happier. How reputable psychologists can believe such a thing is healthy blows my mind.

Can you imagine using a positive *illusion* to fool yourself into happiness? This sounds more like denial than healthy optimism to me. Nonetheless, these researchers are serious about making up positive illusions to help people cope better with life's demands.[1]

My concern is with the term illusion. I am all in favor of a "cheerful optimism," an alternative label that some have used. One can be cheerfully optimistic even when confronted with the most devastating news. It's all a matter of choice. A healthy mind is able to confront the harsh reality of having been fired or of facing major surgery and still maintain an upbeat attitude.

But we don't need optimistic illusions to help us cope with life. What we need is an optimistic facing of truth. Nothing less than the truth, no matter how devastating, can help us make it through tough times. We can rely on God's help in difficulties, but to do so we must be in touch with actuality. God won't help us cope with an illusion.

Positive illusions remind me of a man dying of thirst in the desert who sees, to the left, a mirage of water a mile away. He also sees a real wellspring five miles to the right. The mirage looks more tempting because it is closer, so he chooses it. His illusion may give him the strength to keep going that next mile, but it is not going to save his life. Real wellsprings, although further away, are far more valuable than mirages, no matter how close at hand they may seem.

Balancing Optimism and Reality

Have you heard the one about the optimist who goes into business with a pessimist? Sales are fantastic. At the end of the first three months the optimist declares that their venture has been entirely successful.

"That was a great beginning. People like our product, and sales are increasing every week," the optimist boasts.

"Sure," replies the pessimist, "but if things keep going this way we'll have to order more inventory!"

This story highlights a significant issue. While the pessimist always gets the blame in such stories for pouring cold water on a successful moment, he does accomplish something. In fact, many realists have been accused of pessimism when they are simply trying to help us return to earth.

The pessimist in this story is trying to inject a little reality into the scenario. Of course, he could have waited until the next morning and said, "Isn't it time we ordered more inventory?" That's the difference. The real pessimist can't see any good in anything. The ideal is to be an optimist with both feet on the ground. An optimistic bias is highly desirable. But an optimist who skirts around the truth is in a hazardous state of mind.

Can We Be Too Realistic?

For years psychotherapists have tried to help patients confront the truth, not gloss over it. Nowadays, in some psychotherapeutic circles, there are those who say we need to reconsider too much emphasis on truth. Optimist theorists claim that healthy people naturally downplay the truth, minimize their flaws, and see themselves in a more positive light than can be justified. What people need, these theorists say, is to fudge a little.

This idea assumes that we would all go mad if we knew everything about the real world and how dangerous it really is. For example, in the Los Angeles area where I live, the threat of a devastating earthquake hangs over our heads all the time. One cannot live in constant fear of this, so we fudge a little on the truth and say, "It won't happen to me!"

Where is the balance? There must be equilibrium in our thinking, and this is where the Christian believer has the edge over someone who doesn't believe. The balance comes from seeing life through God's perspective. If we are one of His beloved, we can look the most terrifying reality in the eye and say, "I have a strong consolation because my hope is sure and steadfast, an anchor for my soul" (see Heb. 6:18–19).

Life is often tragic, and some people don't even get a fair shot at it. They get sick. They live in war–torn nations. They barely survive holocausts. Their lives are ruined by scandals. But a sure and steadfast hope doesn't see this life as the end of everything. In fact, it is only the beginning.

Why Tune into Optimism?

Having put the whole topic of optimism in a larger perspective and warned of its excesses, I can now tout its benefits without any further reservations. There is overwhelming research supporting the beneficial effects of optimism—physically, psychologically, and spiritually. The evidence is diverse and extensive.

First, what does optimism do to our bodies? For one thing, it helps us to live longer, even when facing a terminal illness. One study in Great Britain examined sixty–nine women who'd had mastectomies. They were divided into two groups—those who were optimistic and upbeat about their surgery, and those who were down-beat or felt pessimistic. After five years, 75 percent of the pessimists were dead. Less than 25 percent of the optimists had died. Clearly, their frame of mind had an influence over their bodies' ability to fight the cancer.

We don't fully understand the reasons for this, but I have a theory. Pessimism causes more stress to the body than optimism, just as unhappiness is more stressful than happiness. The body, through its incredible mind connection, responds to hopeless feelings as if it is under some great threat. It releases more stress hormones that, in turn, shut down parts of the immune system.

Hans Seligman, a well-known researcher on the topic of helplessness and its effects on the body, discovered that when he measured the disease-fighting cells in the blood of three hundred people (average age seventy-one), those with an optimistic outlook had significantly stronger immune systems. The biochemistry of this connection between an optimistic mind and the workings of the body's immune system is quite remarkable.

In keeping with this theory, studies show that physical health generally can be bettered by donning an optimistic attitude. Optimists report fewer physical problems. Their tolerance for pain is higher, their ability to recover quickly from surgery is faster, and their blood pressure is lower. In fact, there is hardly any physical problem that cannot benefit to some extent from an optimistic boost.

What does optimism do to us psychologically? The effects are obvious. Optimists are happier, more contented, more successful, have greater coping skills, take a more active role in their community, experience less depression, and deal with crises more effectively. And if you need evidence for any of this you are more of a pessimist than you think you are!

Try an experiment if you want to, although I must warn you that it will spoil your day. Find a quiet place where you won't be disturbed. Take your pulse rate. Observe how your body feels. Place your hand against your cheek and note whether your hand is warmer or colder than your face.

Now start to think about everything bad that has happened to you over the past month. Throw in, for good measure, everything bad that has happened to someone else. Think about how awful it all is and how much worse it could get. In fact, try to imagine the absolute worst thing that could possibly happen to you, and keep thinking about it.

Now take your pulse rate again. Is it higher? Put your hand on your face. Does your hand feel colder—a sure sign of stress? Do you feel uncomfortable? Is your mood optimistic or pessimistic? Chances are you have just proven to yourself how powerfully your mind controls your body and mood. Remember this: There is never a thought without a consequence. And if the thought is optimistic, the consequences are better.

Finally, what does optimism do to us spiritually? There is no doubt in my mind that there are two types of Christians: optimistic ones and pessimistic ones. Optimistic Christians have a healthy concept of God, are more likely to pray, use Scripture in uplifting meditations, and have more hope. Pessimistic Christians give up more easily and don't get a lot of joy out of living the Christian life.

Is It Possible to Be Too Optimistic?

Earlier I pointed out how optimism can be distorted. Now let's look at it another way: Is it possible to be too optimistic, even when the optimism is healthy? You must admit this is an intriguing question. After pondering for a while, I must conclude that it *is* possible to be too optimistic, only if by too optimistic we mean not taking action or circumventing other natural processes such as grief or appropriate depression.

Every day in our country, and probably around the world, small and large companies go bankrupt. Why? Because the owners have been overly optimistic. They have looked serious problems or insurmountable obstacles right in the face and said, "I'm optimistic we can find a way around this problem" when they had no idea at all what they were getting into. They simply did not think carefully about the facts before them. They brushed real problems aside and plunged into high-risk situations without a second thought. There is a close connection, therefore, between irresponsible risk-taking and too much optimism. In fact, it is hard to tell the difference.

Sometimes you just have to accept the facts and reconcile yourself to a bleak outcome. No matter how difficult the situation, there is nearly always some good to be found in it, and healthy optimists know how to find silver linings in dark clouds. We hear this in such trite adages as "If life gives you lemons, make lemonade!" But be careful. Not all lemons are worth making into juice. Sometimes we should just throw them away.

I once knew a man in his mid–fifties who had worked as an attorney for a large company and one day got caught in the downsizing of the company and received a pink slip. For two years he tramped the streets looking for a decent job. All he heard was, "You are overqualified," or, "You are not experienced in our type of work." He could have written a book on rejection and how to wallow in it.

In sheer desperation, wanting to be helpful, I found the courage to tell him to try and make lemonade (in the proverbial sense, of course) out of his circumstances. I will never do it again. I'm a quick learner! It was very clear that my advice revealed that I really didn't understand what it is like to be out of a job for such a long time. Over–optimism must never ignore real feelings and should never be used to disregard valid painful circumstances that need to be grieved.

This brings to mind my family's current grief over the tragic death of my son–in–law. Of course we must try to maintain an optimistic outlook for the future, knowing that everyone eventually recovers from grief. But we should never let too much optimism rule the day. It must never be allowed to short-circuit our grieving, nor should it make us feel guilty for our emotional pain.

The Attributes of Optimists

What does it really mean to be a healthy optimist? What attributes can we consider worth cultivating as habits that will breed more optimism into us? The following are worthy of careful and prayerful consideration:

- Healthy optimists do not exaggerate failure.

- Healthy optimists easily change their plans when they don't work.

- Healthy optimists try to interpret rejection in a positive light.

- Healthy optimists turn criticism into food for growth.

- Healthy optimists turn little blessings into big boosters.

- Healthy optimists don't take themselves too seriously.

Martin Seligman of the University of Pennsylvania, famous for his work on "learned helplessness," now uses the phrase "learned optimism." His research shows that in as little as one sixteen-hour training workshop, university freshmen who were selected for being excessively pessimistic were able to transform their attitudes into more optimistic ones.[2] They worked primarily on learning how to dispute their chronic negative thoughts and shape social and work skills that were more optimistic. Following up eighteen months later, many had kept these newfound skills. Optimism had been learned as a habit.

Hope—God's Plan for Optimism

What does the Bible have to say about optimism? While the word itself is not used in Scripture, there is a close relative worth highlighting here. The biblical word for optimism is *hope*, although there are some important differences between the two concepts. I cannot conclude this chapter without commenting on these differences and pointing the reader to a more complete optimism—optimism that incorporates the hope God has planted in us through Jesus Christ.

As we've seen, optimism generally refers to a tendency to take the most hopeful view of circumstances. In common parlance, it is looking on the bright side of things. Hope is deeper than this. It looks at bad circumstances and believes that they have a purpose. It desires to see some good come of terrible tragedies. Hope also implies some confidence in the future, no matter how gloomy it may appear to be. So, if I say, "I hope to go to heaven," I am not just being an optimist; I'm trusting in some very important promises. My hope of going to heaven is not just a matter of looking on the bright side of a bad world and hoping for the best. My hope for heaven is fact-based. It has been promised to me (see Titus 2:13–14). All I need to obtain hope is faith.

Hoping that something will happen is more like optimism than the hope presented in Scripture. In fact, just hoping for something is inferior to optimism. It is probably one of the evils in the world, if taken too far. My grandchildren often engage in hoping. They hope we'll go to the movies. They hope we will play a game. They hope that Daddy will come home quickly so they can start the party. *Hoping* here is synonymous with *wishing*, and they are just expressing what they really, really, really wish would happen. I suppose wishing has a large dose of optimism driving it, but it is not the optimism that comes from hope. True hope is born of the knowledge that God, not random chance, is in control, and that He cares.

Optimism that stems from such hope, clearly taught to us in Scripture, is more effective than optimism based simply on wishful thinking or clever psychological fabrication. It has a solid foundation in reality—God's reality. It is born of the deep assurance that God has promised His abiding presence both in life and in death.

One of my favorite hymns is Edward Mote's "The Solid Rock." Based on 1 Corinthians 3:11, the second verse always brings tears to my eyes and hope to my breast:

> *When darkness veils His lovely face,*
> *I rest on His unchanging grace;*
> *In ev'ry high and stormy gale*
> *My anchor holds within the veil.*
> *On Christ, the solid Rock, I stand;*
> *All other ground is sinking sand,*
> *All other ground is sinking sand.*

Optimism born of this true hope can never be overturned. It will see you through life's darkest valleys. It will lead you on to tomorrow's spectacular sunrise.

CHAPTER 12

HABIT #8:
ACCEPT YOURSELF FOR WHO YOU ARE

*It is not an easy world to live in. It is not an easy
world to be decent in. It is not an easy world to
understand oneself in, nor to like oneself in. But it
must be lived in, and in the living there is one
person you absolutely have to be with—(yourself).*
Jo Coudert
Advice from a Failure

I remember reading a story about a self–conscious, shy, and
awkward child named Margaret Runbeck. She described how,
by persistent scholarship and a lot of good fortune, she found
herself on the platform during her high–school commencement
exercises, waiting to give the valedictory address. She could not
recall what had come over her when she agreed to undertake
this menacing task, since she was normally a retiring person who
shunned the limelight.

Margaret recounted how, with her speech churning in her
frightened head, she somehow found enough courage to face the
sea of blurred faces in the school auditorium. Her father was
there. He had taken a precious day's leave from work to attend, a
leave he really couldn't afford to take. But nothing was going to
keep the proud father from hearing his daughter make her speech.

Her mother was there. Traveling to the auditorium, Margaret
remembered looking at her mother's hands and noting that her
one forefinger still bore the marks of pinpricks from the many
stitches it had taken to handmake Margaret's graduation dress.

119

Her grandparents were there also. They had traveled quite a distance in a very unreliable car to take part in this triumphant moment.

But all Margaret could think about was her impending disgrace. She was sure she would embarrass everyone. And how would they ever forgive her for failing to meet their expectations?

To make matters worse, Margaret was to sit next to the speaker who had been invited to deliver the commencement address. Her English teacher had told her quite firmly that she was to chat cordially with the distinguished man beforehand. "Don't let him feel left out," was her instruction, spelled out in tones that implied terrible consequences if she failed.

But where was the speaker? Margaret recalled becoming even more nervous because he was late. Margaret stared at the empty chair next to her. It seemed so menacing. What ogre was going to sit himself down there and embarrass her even more? She tried not to look around—it always helps not to look at others at times like this. If you don't see people, you can pretend that they're not there.

The speaker finally arrived and sat down beside her. At first he didn't notice her. Not to be deterred from keeping her promise to her English teacher, Margaret somehow managed to open the conversation. "Just be yourself," she said silently in her heart, not knowing where that idea came from. What came out was: "Sir, I'm supposed to talk with you, be witty and all that, but . . . but . . . I don't know what to say; I'm scared to death."

The distinguished-looking gentleman glanced up from his notes, studied her for a moment, then said, "I'm scared too. I don't think my speech is that good. I don't think I'm going to go over all that well." He glanced back at his notes for a few moments while he sized up the situation. Here was a young girl who thought she was the only awkward person in the world. She wasn't. And as Margaret stared at him she realized that he was feeling awkward too. Her outlook began to improve.

"I'll tell you a secret," he finally said. "And if you follow it, you'll never ever be scared again. Everyone on earth is a little self-conscious and unsure of himself, just like you and me. So, when you meet someone, take a minute to first make the other person feel comfortable, just as you did with me. If you do, you'll never suffer from self-consciousness again."

Margaret could never remember exactly what happened after that. She did recall feeling very happy when it was all over and thinking that the whole occasion was wonderful. Most importantly, she never forgot the advice she got that day from a man she didn't know and never saw personally again. But she used the lesson she learned that day a thousand times over: Always make the other person feel comfortable first, and you will begin to forget your own self-consciousness.

As the years passed, Margaret remained grateful to the man and often wished she could remember who he was so she could tell him of her gratitude. One day, when she was much older, she was clearing out her attic. Bits of trivia and memorabilia had been hoarded there through the years. Suddenly she came across her high-school commencement-day program, and her heart skipped a beat. Perhaps it would tell her the name of the special guest who had helped her gain the freedom to be herself.

There it was in large bold print: "Commencement Address, by the Honorable Franklin D. Roosevelt, Assistant Secretary of the Navy." Margaret was astounded. Roosevelt had been quite young when he sat beside her on that platform, and she had not connected him with the powerful man who led the United States of America through World War II. No wonder his advice had been so wise.

An Opportunity for Self-Discovery

We can all benefit from a life-changing moment like Margaret's, and the earlier the better. I think all of us fear being "discovered" for what we really are, because we assume that people won't like us if they see our true selves. Fortunately, that's not true. The sooner we let people see who we really are, the sooner we will be set free from our self-made prisons of self-consciousness.

Franklin D. Roosevelt taught Margaret several important lessons that day. First, he encouraged her to remove the focus from herself and to give attention to someone else's uneasiness. When you try to make things a little more comfortable for them, you'll be helping yourself also.

Perhaps the greater lesson, however, was that until she could feel comfortable in just being herself, Margaret would always be penalized by her self-consciousness. She had to come to the place of total self-acceptance or she would never be free. Without settling that matter with herself, she would be forever hounded by the expectations of others and by her fear of what they might think and say.

What Does Being Yourself Really Mean?

Many Christians have difficulty with the whole notion of "being yourself," so permit me to clarify what I think that means. Being yourself is not a matter of self-centeredness nor of asserting yourself over others. It is certainly not a determination to do it your way.

I've always disliked the sentiment behind the words of the song made famous by Frank Sinatra, "I Did It My Way." I think it sends the wrong message, especially to those who are Christians and know how much havoc we can create by going our own way. But I do want to be myself, and you do me a great injustice if you tell me I can't. If I am not allowed to be myself then who am I to be? You? If I am to fulfill the calling that God has placed in my heart, I can only do so if I claim the freedom to be myself. I can't be Billy Graham, or John Stott, or William Carey, or any other great Christian leader you care to mention. I can only be myself, Arch Hart.

And I must be myself in *truth*. I love this expression. It reminds me that there is to be no false modesty, no shamming. I must accept the truth about who I am, flaws and strengths, and learn to live in harmony with these traits. If I don't take the good and the bad together, God cannot fulfill His plan for my life.

I have a great compassion for pastors. In fact I focus most of my speaking on pastors' groups because I feel I have something to offer clergymen, who have rightly been called "the Walking Wounded." Being a pastor is as emotionally demanding as any vocation I know. God and God alone gives many of them the strength and courage to keep doing what they do. Never under-estimate the demanding complexity of your pastor's duties.

One aspect of ministry that makes it emotionally hazardous is the restriction we place on pastors with regard to being real. This is particularly true among conservative, evangelically inclined believers. Pastors are constantly bombarded with expectations about who they must be. They feel they cannot let down their guard and be human. Parishioners won't let them. They must be perfect. No mistakes.

Congregations put these men on pedestals and then either revere them with compliments or pelt them with criticisms. This is why most pastors experience a slow erosion of their self-esteem in ministry, even if they appear to be successful on the outside. They are not allowed to be flawed like the rest of us, or at least that is the message we send them.

Not only do well-intentioned Christian people not allow pastors to be themselves, they deny their fellow Christians this right as well. Ask those who suffer from depression whether they feel accepted by fellow Christians. Most of them wouldn't dare tell anyone else that they need to be on an antidepressant medication. They'd be hounded out of fellowship.

Hurting people rarely mention their pain in their churches, knowing too well that they will be branded as failures. So instead of opening themselves to support and help, they retreat into guilt and try to appear as strong as the others. They aren't free to be themselves. Yet, for centuries, wise believers have recognized the importance of personal authenticity. It was Erasmus who said, "It is the chiefest point of happiness that man is willing to be what he is."

What Does It Take to Be Yourself?

Please understand that what I mean about being yourself is nothing more than accepting who God has made you to be. It is not a matter of doing your own thing. That's what adolescents do because it's their way of achieving their individuality. Being yourself never involves dominating others or disregarding their feelings.

I've heard these distortions often enough: "I'm just going to speak my mind. People need to know where I'm coming from. I just want to be myself!" What they really mean when they say this is, "I'm tired of being a good person; I just want to show my ugly side as a way of punishing everyone I don't like."

Being yourself in truth is quite the opposite. The more you are genuinely yourself, the more you respect the rights of others. You stop pretending that you are someone you are not. You stop being afraid of not meeting the expectations of others. It's not that you don't care what they think—of course you do. You just don't let fear direct your life. You direct it yourself. That way, when you stand before God to give a full account of your life, you can do so without having to confess that you lived to please others rather than living solely to please Him.

What does it take to be yourself? I could probably write a book on this topic alone, but for now, here are four important steps.

1. Stop Comparing Yourself with Others

I am strongly of the opinion that 95 percent of us wish, deep down, that we were someone else. There are a few who say that they have never felt this way, but when I push them, they concede that they may have at one time or another indulged such a fantasy. I have tested this theory over many years and have found it to be true—very few people are completely satisfied with who they are.

People indulge the fantasy of being someone else. Evangelists want to be like Billy Graham, preachers want to be like Charles Hadden Spurgeon, girls long to be glamorous movie stars, and boys wish they were great football players. We call these role models "heroes," and we idolize them and aspire to be like them. Too many men and women constantly compare themselves to others to see if they're smarter, taller, thinner, wiser, or more passionate, skillful, artistic, charismatic, or lovable. (I stopped with lovable because I was beginning to feel like a thesaurus.) Psychologists call this "impression monitoring," and the label speaks for itself.

We need to break the habit of comparing ourselves to others and trying to pattern ourselves after them. I find it helpful to remind myself just how unique every person is. The other evening I was listening to Jimmy Durante, the comedian-singer of a few generations back. I've always had a fondness for this man. I grew up listening to his gravel voice and seeing his protruding nose on cinema screens.

What was Durante's appeal? He was unlike anyone else before him, and people loved him for it. He didn't become famous because he cloned himself after somebody else. If he had tried to be like Eddie Cantor or Al Jolson he would have seemed ridiculous. Instead he was himself, gravel voice, schnoz and all, and that's what people loved!

In the same sense, you've got to believe that there is only one of you. And being who YOU are—in truth—is the greatest thing you have to offer this world. No reproductions of someone else, please! People will love you for being yourself more than for being perfect or for imitating someone else.

2. Celebrate Who You Are

Accepting ourselves as we are is only a part of the process of moving toward being ourselves. But there's more. The next step is to celebrate who you are. Here again Christians have some difficulty understanding what is required. To celebrate yourself seems a little like self-aggrandizement or boasting, and it can be so, if it is done in a narcissistic way. But narcissism isn't what I am talking about here. What I mean is that we need to stop being ashamed or embarrassed by who we are. We need to stand tall in our own skins and hold our heads high.

Not having the courage to be yourself has one serious consequence: You forfeit the opportunity to become what you have the potential to become. Arthur Schopenhauer, the German philosopher, believed that humans forfeit three-fourths of their potential just because they try to be like other people. I agree with him. And what amazes me is that he saw this more than a hundred years ago. For generations, people have destroyed personal potential by not being willing to accept and celebrate themselves.

Not only do we forfeit a large part of ourselves, but we forfeit the potential of what God has in mind for us to be. How can we fulfill God's plan for us when we keep sidestepping the blueprints drawn up specifically for us? God's sovereign design for others won't work for us—it was designed to include their individuality, not ours. We need to embrace our own blueprints.

3. Don't Take Yourself Too Seriously

Suppose you feel guilty about a faux pas you made at a dinner party. Or your new hairstyle didn't come out just as you wanted it to. Or the boss ridicules something you did at work. Maybe you came in last in a race, and your friends made fun of it. Maybe you spilled water all over the table at lunch. So what? The world is not going to change because of anything you may or may not have done.

We take ourselves too seriously. What we do on a daily basis clearly is not the most important thing in the universe. Yet we often react emotionally to our little misadventures as if they were. Setbacks, humiliating moments, and disappointments— life is full of them. Unless we lighten up we will never achieve abiding happiness.

What we should all do is something a well-known professor has done. He has a mirror on his office wall that he uses to comb his hair before going to class. Underneath the mirror is a little sign that says:

This person is not to be taken too seriously.

Abraham Lincoln had a reputation for not taking himself too seriously, especially his appearance. He told this story to describe his view of himself:

"Sometimes I feel like the ugly man who met an old woman traveling through a forest. The old woman says, 'You are the ugliest man I ever saw.'

"The ugly man replies, 'I can't help it.'

"'No, I guess not,' the woman admits, 'but the least you could do is to stay home!'"

Part of not taking ourselves too seriously is being able to laugh at ourselves. Laughing at our foibles and mistakes helps us become more candid and self-accepting. The person who can generally laugh at his or her failures is able to learn from them more effectively than the person who thinks failures are the end of the world. "End of the world" thinking always inhibits discovery.

Laughing at ourselves also helps us to feel more in control. We don't blame others for our mistakes; we own them readily, and we move on comfortably. By taking ourselves lightly, we stop believing that life owes us a favor. A healthy sense of humor is also a great stress reliever, a valve that lets off steam.

Humor is not only a great coping mechanism, but established research shows it to be a stimulant to our immune system, so we live healthier lives. Of course the Bible has been saying that for centuries. Proverbs 15:13 advises, "A merry heart maketh a cheerful countenance." Proverbs 17:22 agrees: "A merry heart doeth good like a medicine."

I suggest you lighten up, laugh at your mistakes, and let the world see your beautiful smile!

4. Work Hard at Liking Yourself

There is a scene in *Alice in Wonderland* where the duchess says to Alice, "Be what you would seem to be—or, if you'd like it put more simply—never imagine yourself not to be otherwise than what it might appear to others that what you were or might have been was not otherwise than what you had been would have appeared to them to be otherwise." Poor Alice! What sense was she to make of this? Well, simply stated, the duchess is telling Alice to just be herself, and like it! You are only special if you are yourself.

The more we are just ourselves, the less we are like everyone else, and this is very important to God. If He wanted us all to be clones of each other, He could have created us with the same appearance. We would all be the same height, weight, have the same shaped mouths and ears, share the same physiques, and walk the same walk. He could also have made us with the same sense of humor, taste in music, and love of spinach. But He didn't. No two people on earth are alike.

So what does it mean to like yourself? Does it mean you sit and adore yourself in front of the mirror? I hope not. Does it mean you are so perfectly content with who you are that you see no reason to grow? Absolutely not. But we Christians have a particular reason to learn this important lesson. I can understand an unbeliever saying, "I can never like myself; I am just too bad a person for anyone to like." But we are in Christ. And we need to begin changing our attitudes about ourselves. If He loved us before we knew or loved Him, surely we can learn to see ourselves as lovable.

Liking yourself is nothing more than not hating yourself anymore. And hating yourself is like having a demon on your shoulder. Every time you do something wrong, the demon screams "You are not worthy! You must hate yourself!" For some people, this habit is extremely incapacitating. They come to believe that unless they hate themselves continually, they're not being spiritual.

Do we resist liking ourselves because God doesn't like us? Hardly. He made us, loved us, died for us, and lives for us. He is not likely to dislike us, particularly if we have accepted Him into our lives. I believe we resist the idea of self-acceptance because there has been a long history of Christian teaching that wallows in self-rejection. For generations, Christian culture has reinforced false humility and superficial righteousness.

Feeling a Little Odd

Besides wishing we were someone else or hating ourselves for wrong theological reasons, I have also observed that most of us resist liking ourselves because we fear we are a little odd.

We can't like ourselves because we don't think others can like us for who we are. We feel like eccentric misfits in a world that is committed to conformity.

Earlier in this book I mentioned that I took my daughter Sharon to see the stage version of *Beauty and the Beast* at the Schubert Theater. That story spoke to us in many ways, and one of them had to do with this very issue. Near the beginning of the play, Belle, the heroine, asks her father, "Papa, do you think I'm odd?" She stands out from the rest of the villagers because she reads books.

Surprised, her father replies, "No, Belle, you're not odd!" He reminds her that she is her mother's daughter, and therefore she is "class." He tells her that while the others are the common herd, she is unique, the "crème de la crème." No matter what she does, he's on her side. Most of all he loves her, and that's all that matters!

There I was, sitting next to my own daughter, who had been left bereaved at such a young age. She had been wondering the very same thing—had tragedy made her "odd"? It was a very emotional moment for both of us.

What about you? Do you feel a little odd? If so, take heart. No matter how unique you are, you have a heavenly Father who loves you. He made you just the way He wanted you to be. He is committed to you, your growth, and your future. What a wonderful father He is! When you think about it, what else matters?

CHAPTER 13

HABIT #9: STAY IN TOUCH WITH REALITY

There is no greater disaster in the spiritual life
than to be immersed in unreality.
Thomas Merton
Thoughts in Solitude

At thirty-two years of age, Nancy has given up on life. She is convinced that there is no God, no purpose, and no hope. She sees no prospect for a happy and fulfilling future. All she envisions doing is enduring what is to come, or better still, finding a way to get out of the life business as soon as possible.

During her first therapy session with me, Nancy spoke of abandoned relationships, shattered ambitions, and excruciatingly lonely nights. Nothing she had dreamed of for her life had materialized; every dream she had ever imagined had been shattered.

Her present state of mind had begun three years before when she was employed by a large organization as a sales manager. Through diligence and hard work she had made her way up the ladder of promotion, past others older than she, and was soon competing very effectively in a field traditionally dominated by men.

At first she'd found her work satisfying. It had occupied most of her waking mind and given her a sense of fulfillment. She had dated some, but had not met the right man yet. "There's still lots of time for this," she had reassured herself while she was ladder-climbing. Then things began to go wrong. She became restless and unhappy. Seeds of discontentment emerged. Her life, which was once a beautiful garden, was now growing weeds. Beauty gave way to ugliness.

The Hazards of Wrong Beliefs

It all started when she read a well-known book on how to improve your life. I won't mention the title—it doesn't deserve any free publicity. "Health, wealth, and success belong to every-one," the book said. "Whatever and whoever you are, you can be more successful." It went on to say that God wants everyone to be wealthy and successful, and if you serve Him, think His thoughts, and dream His dreams, success can be yours. What's wrong with these ideas? Perhaps you've heard them yourself so many times that you, too, have come to believe them.

Well, there are many things wrong with this message. To begin with, it fails to mention that most success is built upon a mountain of failure. And, oh yes, it says nothing about how much hard work it takes to be really successful. Interestingly, success soothsayers often leave the part about hard work and persistence out of their formulas.

Nancy became obsessed with the idea that she wasn't being as successful as she could be and that she deserved a better deal from life. She became profoundly dissatisfied with herself and her circumstances. She decided that she had settled for the clouds when the stars were her destiny. And as far as she could see, even her clouds were nothing more than ground fog.

So Nancy resigned her position as sales manager and set out to conquer the world of prosperity. Six months later she was deeply depressed. She was unable to find a job that matched her skills, and before long she had spent all her savings and was on the verge of bankruptcy. Her parents had helped her all they could, and she would have to deal alone with having no job prospects, no husband, no family of her own, no future. Every-thing seemed hopeless.

When I first encountered her, Nancy remained sequestered in her apartment, withdrawn from all social contacts. Brooding had become her major pastime. She felt dejected, defeated, and dis-traught. How did Nancy end up in such a sorry state? She lost touch with reality. And I don't mean she was psychotic. She had simply bought into a series of erroneous ideas that had distorted her belief system. The idea that it was God's will that everyone should be financially prosperous and personally successful had become an obsession. Because she believed this, she behaved accordingly—such is the power of our beliefs.

That particular teaching, extremely common today, is a distortion of God's promises to His children. While we are called to live an abundant life, the abundance God promises has more to do with spiritual prosperity than with worldly riches. But today's success-and-prosperity preachers fail to recognize this.

In Need of Reality-Based Beliefs

Speaking as a Christian psychologist who has tried to help believers achieve healthier emotions, I would say that there is no greater potential for disaster in any aspect of life—physical, psychological, or spiritual—than to be immersed in unreality or fantasy. Our beliefs must be rooted on solid rock. When we feed off unreality we die, because unreality provides no substance capable of sustaining us. Unreality, and beliefs that are based on unreality, are nothing more than that mirage we talked about before, appearing in a dry and dusty desert. Mirages give the illusion that there is beauty and growth, but the nearer you get to them, the further away they move. And when you put a mirage to the test of life, it vanishes altogether.

Our world fosters unreality and presents it to us as if it were truth. Movies, novels, TV, and even some preachers promise us distorted and unrealistic pictures of love, life, affluence, and tri-umph. We live our lives as if they were one long fantasy. And when these beliefs don't deliver what they promise, we sink into a deep, though often unconscious, resentment because we believe that God is unfair. Someone else always has it better than us.

As a result, contentment is a rare quality in our twentieth-century evangelical Christendom. The experience of the apostle

Paul, who said, "I have learned in whatsoever state I am, there-with to be content" (Phil. 4:11), is seldom seen nowadays. The reason? It is difficult to be satisfied when you are surrounded by an artificial world, caught up in a system of beliefs which are fostered by unreality.

Give Yourself the Gift of Reality

One of the greatest gifts you can give yourself is the gift of reality. If you really want to be a contented person, make it a habit to always be in touch with truth. Jean Tostand, the French biologist and writer, once said, "I prefer the honest jargon of reality to the outright lies of books." He was referring to novels—perhaps these days we should add movies and TV.

Changing circumstances, occasional disappointments, growing old, and eventually dying—all these give life a new significance when we fully accept them at face value. Every minute becomes precious. You don't spend time wishing that things were different or escaping into a fantasy. Once we appreciate life for what it really is, we discover a new thrill in being alive.

Fred was my patient many years ago, and he was on the verge of suicide. His life, like Nancy's, was a total wreck. At thirty-six years of age he had experienced nothing but pain and unmitigated misery. When he was sixteen, Fred was erroneously diagnosed as a paranoid schizophrenic because he didn't trust anyone, and because he'd had a series of angry encounters with schoolteachers. For many years afterward he was treated, albeit quite unsuccessfully because of an incorrect diagnosis, by a series of psychiatrists and psychologists.

Fred wanted to make a success of his life. He yearned to be a whole person. He was an intelligent man, and in fact, he eventually went on to complete two master's degrees. But he couldn't come to terms with who he was as a person. His periodic outbursts of rage, we discovered, were always related to his desire to be someone else. He just would not accept the reality of who he was—looks, height, personality, whatever. In fact, Fred would spend countless hours lying on his bed fantasizing that he was a great business tycoon or a movie star.

Our therapy focused on helping Fred accept reality. He was the person God had made—freckles, lumps, and all the other imperfections that precluded his looking like a Hollywood idol. Fred had to come to grips with the truth that there was no way he could not be himself, short of quitting life. Life is not a fairy tale that changes frogs into handsome princes. Frogs stay frogs. And frogs better accept being frogs because there is no other life for them.

Slowly, Fred came to understand and accept this. Reluctantly, he began to like himself a little. With his new reality, Fred gradually gained a deeper sense of personal satisfaction.

Reality Thinking

The healthy habit of confronting reality is what I call "reality thinking." By consistently forcing yourself to ask the question: "What is reality here?" and then seeking to engage it with all the courage you can muster, you slowly make it a habit of your mind.

The idea of reality thinking is not at cross-purposes with other healthy behaviors such as positive or possibility thinking. But it does take our thought process one step further. Not only is it more consistent with our modern understanding of the value of cognitive approaches to therapy, but it is a more constructive and biblically sound way of thinking.

Reality thinking encourages individuals to attain their full potential by unshackling their constricted minds from negative patterns that are self-limiting. It stresses that all thinking must be based on reality and that thinking must be sensible and logical.

There is one central goal in reality thinking: to maximize our potential for fulfilling God's plan for our lives. It seeks to remove every hindrance to finding out what God's plan is and discovering how to achieve it. Reality thinking recognizes the inhibiting influences of bad early-childhood training and seeks to undo the negativity that so often breeds feelings of defeat and helplessness.

The Ingredients of Reality Thinking

Reality thinking brings together three very important truths:

1. First, the Gospel releases us to be ourselves. Christ has set us free from sin's destruction and power and from the terror of our mortality.

We have a finite number of years to our existence. Although we all know this, most of us behave as if we are going to live forever. We also know that there is more to existence than this life, yet we all live as if nothing else mattered. To keep in touch with eternity is to keep in touch with the reality of this world. Eternity keeps this mortal life in proper perspective.

2. Second, reality thinking inhibits the influence of negative and defeatist thinking. Drs. Peale and Schuller are correct. Most of us are limited and restricted by negative thoughts. We must break free from helpless and hopeless habits of behavior. Artificial fences of pessimism keep us locked in dry and barren feeding grounds. These fences can be broken down; many of them are only illusions.

3. Third, reality thinking makes us aware of the limitations of a finite world. Nothing is to be gained by ignoring reality, and all thinking that distorts or denies the realities of life is deceptive. There is danger in teaching people how to think of unlimited possibilities, to use success-generating imagination and obstacle-overcoming visual strategies. The truth is, some expectations cannot be fulfilled because of certain reality-based limitations. If your dreams are tied to reality, then these strategies free you to achieve your dreams. If they are not, you are courting disaster.

Reality thinking helps us to explore all possibilities, encourages positive rather than negative ideas, and taps the resources of God's limitless power. But it also encourages us to keep our feet on the ground and stay in touch with reality—reality as God defines it.

Reality Thinking Is Not Impulsive

Public Television's *Masterpiece Theater* once told the story of World War II soldiers who disarmed unexploded bombs during the London Blitz. Imagine a soldier disarming an unexploded bomb. He looks at it all over, trying to discover where the fuse mechanism is, knowing that the Nazis frequently changed the location of the fuses. Often a bomb disposal officer, young and operating on instinct, was confronted with a new fuse, different from any other he had seen before.

With a life expectancy of only weeks once they accepted this dangerous assignment, only commissioned officers were allowed to tackle the task. Ordinary soldiers couldn't be trusted. So a young officer, new to the war, studied his first unexploded bomb. He was left alone to tackle the defusing—why sacrifice more than one man at a time? He asked himself, "Should I try to remove the fuse the way they taught me? What if it doesn't behave like the others I've seen?"

Clear procedures had been worked out for every bomb the Nazis had devised thus far, and any new bomb discovered was supposed to be carefully researched and the changes documented. No one was to take unnecessary risks. Yet many of these young soldiers looked at a strange fuse and believed they could do the job of defusing it anyway. Extreme danger doesn't always make one more cautious. When all seems hopeless anyway, carelessness often steps in. Many young men lost their lives simply because they were impulsive.

The human mind easily succumbs to impulsive responses. It is part of our refusal to confront reality. We escape from reality by acting without forethought. The senior officers in charge of bomb disposal had to continuously weed out impulsive soldiers who couldn't stay in touch with reality. It was safer to use terrified men to diffuse bombs than those who were both fearless and foolish.

Taking unnecessary risks through impulsive behavior is not reality-based thinking. It is quite the opposite—absurd and crazy. Yet from time to time we all do it.

Reality Thinking Is Positive

Some people object to the whole idea of reality thinking, believing that it is too negative. These critics equate reality with downbeat, hard-nosed, killjoy dispositions where to be in touch with reality means you're not allowed to have any fun. "Reality is a prison," they say, "from which we must escape. The real world is too dangerous and uncertain, so give us liberty from its miseries."

Nothing could be further from the truth. Reality thinking is always positive if the circumstances are appropriate. It stares truth right in the eyes, allowing us to find constructive and liberating ways to deal with it. Reality thinking is not always positive in the sense that it refuses to overlook or deny the actual negatives of life.

To think realistically means that when confronted by a troublesome or anxiety-producing situation, instead of looking for a way to distort the facts, we accept them for what they are. And we do so with the most positive perspective the facts will allow. We realistically evaluate all aspects, both positive and negative.

People who are only willing to look at the positive and persistently ignore the negative are deluding themselves. They are trying to believe that their situation is not as bad as it really is. For them, reality doesn't exist. They may temporarily feel better, but the real problem does not go away.

I once helped a couple work through a difficult life decision. Paul, the husband, was in his mid-forties and had become thoroughly bored with his life as an engineer. He wanted to make a change to a more exciting and demanding work situation. One day he heard that a business was for sale and tried to convince his wife that they should sell their home, take their savings, buy the business, and move to New York.

Carol, Paul's wife, refused to go along with the idea. She was convinced that it was a bad decision. There was too much risk involved. Paul accused Carol of having no faith. Of course, what he should have said was, "You have no faith in me." But he made it sound as if she had no faith in God.

Both Paul and Carol had prayed diligently about the matter. She said God had told her no. He claimed God was telling him yes. They both told stories of how God had spoken to them through selected Scriptures or personal incidents. It always amazes me how easily we rearrange the facts to fit what we want to see or hear. The question remained, who was right? The conflict was destroying their marriage.

As we explored the issue together, it became clear that Paul, in his eagerness to make a change, was looking at the whole deal far too positively. Often in his past, he had made mistakes by refusing to be objective about negative facts. There were obvious blind spots in the way he was looking at the proposed venture, yet he dismissed as petty all his wife's arguments against going. "Carol is too realistic," he said sarcastically. "She never wants to take risks."

I saw Carol differently. She seemed to have a good business head on her shoulders. She knew about cash–flow problems, carrying too much debt, and so on. Paul, on the other hand, was far too impatient and had not taken the time to check out other prospects.

After clarifying all the issues with me, they compromised. Paul agreed to at least look realistically at some other possibilities. One week later they returned to see me, both smiling broadly. Within days of our counseling session, they heard about another business offer. The terms were infinitely better, the risks less, and they didn't have to move from their home. They were now united in believing that they were making the right decision to purchase this business. Forcing Carol and Paul—mainly Paul—to think realistically prevented a disaster. It usually does.

This is not to say that reality thinking never takes risks. Of course it does. But it does not gamble on achieving success when the odds are hopeless. Intelligent risk-taking is not the same as gambling. When you gamble, you are not sure you know all the facts. You are like a bungee–cord jumper who hasn't checked to see whether the cord is properly attached. This is stupidity. No amount of positive thinking will overcome obstacles over which you have no control. If you fail to look at all the obstacles and check all the ties before you take your plunge, don't be surprised if you fail, and fail dramatically.

Please remember that God is the God of order, not disorder. When two people earnestly seek His guidance on a life–changing decision, for it to be God's clear guidance each needs to have peace regarding the issue. God's guidance must create unity. God does not solve one mistake with another. When there is no unity, I always suspect that unreal thinking is getting in the way for one of the parties.

Reality Thinking Takes Control

Life has a way of turning us into victims. A victim is one who has been cheated or has suffered at the hands of others. Victims have not only suffered crimes, they have also suffered neglect. Victims suffer whenever they find themselves under the control of other people or circumstances. They never feel that they control their own destiny. There are a lot of people around who believe that they are victims.

Under Christ, we should be in control of ourselves. Since we are responsible for our own lives and will eventually give an account to God, we cannot allow others to determine our beliefs, actions, or feelings. It is imperative that we free ourselves of the manipulations and controls of everyone except God. Of course this is not easy. We are conditioned by our need to please others, and we easily surrender control to them. The wages are small, but somehow, pleasing others seems to pay more handsomely than pleasing ourselves.

Reality thinking is a way of removing ourselves from the trap of victimization. To think realistically demands that we stop being controlled by what others think. It requires us to take control of our own destiny, actions, and reactions. This way we can feel free to do what we believe God wants us to do, not in blatant disregard for the feelings of others, but in a spirit of gentleness and kindness.

When you are in control, under God, you will find a new joy in the actions of self-sacrifice. You cannot sacrifice that which is not yours to give. Only when you know that your life belongs to you and is not under the control of others can you really feel free to sacrifice it in love's service.

Reality Thinking Puts God in Control

Perhaps the greatest benefit of reality thinking as a habit is that it maximizes the likelihood that you will keep God in control. All forms of escape, whether the excessive use of denial, positivism, or negativism, take us out of God's will simply because they are not truthful. God can only help us if we stay in touch with reality. For this reason, the habit of always looking at the real issues of your life can prevent your wandering off the pathway of God's design for you.

Reality is not something to be avoided. Reality is a question of perspective; the further we get away from it, the more it distorts our lives. There is only one way to really live successfully in this world, and it requires us to be in constant touch with truth. Whose truth can we trust? Only God's. The miracle is, God's truth transforms everything it touches.

CHAPTER 14

HABIT #10:
CHERISH GOD'S LOVE AND WISDOM

We give credit to human wisdom when we
should give credit to the Divine guidance of
God through childlike people who were foolish
enough to trust God's wisdom and the
supernatural equipment of God.
Oswald Chambers

When I was in my mid–teens, a Christian friend gave me a book to read that shook my young mind to the core. It changed my life and left me forever the better for it. The book was Charles Sheldon's novel *In His Steps*. It moved me deeply and was one of the instruments that brought me to Christ at about the time I left high school.

As a young sixteen–year–old my life was confused. I was un–happy and ready to receive whatever direction might hold hope for a better life. The message of that book struck home at a deep level. I gave my life to Christ publicly at the first opportunity after reading it, which was an evangelistic service conducted by a preacher from England who was visiting South Africa, the Reverend Ivor Powell.

The part of that book that has stayed with me down through the years is this question: "What would Jesus do?" It is the question around which the whole novel revolves. Following a moment of renewal in the pastor's life, he and five other people in the story have embarked upon a yearlong experience in Christianity. As they confront life's complex dilemmas, each has agreed to conduct his or her life according to that one simple question: What would

Jesus do? How they answer the question for themselves has momentous consequences for each of them. Their lives were made or shattered, depending on how they responded.

For months after reading the book, I was haunted with the question it asked. Even today, about forty-five years later, I still consider it when I am faced with a difficult decision or a conflict of values. *What would Jesus do?* I have not always answered wisely or done what my heart has told me to do. But when I have, it has been revolutionary.

Many of my patients through the years have also learned to ask this question. What would Jesus do if His child were causing all that trouble at school? What would He do if His neighbor's dog created a disturbance? What would He do if His boss was crabby and always picking on Him? What would He do if His sermon was criticized by a senior elder or if someone didn't like the way He dressed? It's a simple enough question. The predicament lies in finding the right answer.

Asking this question prayerfully and then acting on the answer can have a powerful impact on your life. "What would Jesus do?" is one way to ascertain the wisdom of God, wisdom we all need desperately in these confusing days. And asking for this wisdom is quite acceptable. The apostle James assures us of this in James 1:5. I particularly favor the Living Bible's version of it. "If you want to know what God wants you to do, ask him, and he will gladly tell you, for he is always ready to give a bountiful supply of wisdom to all who ask him; he will not resent it."

If you want to have a healthy mind, you must be willing to obey James' advice.

The Craving for Right Direction

E. Stanley Jones, the famous author and missionary to India, writes that there is an inherent and basic urge in all of us to go beyond ourselves. What he means is that we all have a craving to know the right direction. Most of us have learned the hard way how easily we can lose our way. We realize that we need direction from outside.

Built into the very fabric of our humanness is a need for orientation. And we also crave growth. I clearly recall wanting to grow as a child—not just to be older and bigger, but to grow in the sense of moving on into new things. If we are to grow, we must grow in the right direction. Otherwise the growth is disastrous.

Here is the key question: Who do we turn to for the right direction? Our world is confused by countless voices clamoring to be our authority. Yet the only voice worth listening to is the voice of God. Psychology has far more questions than answers. Philosophy doesn't even know where the starting gate is. And as far as politicians are concerned, get serious! But the voice of God is loud and clear and has been made known to us through Christ and His Word.

Our craving to know the right direction is trustworthy. It was planted in our souls by the One who created us and is part and parcel of our human nature, which means that it is inescapable. To be a healthy thinker, we must allow ourselves to form the habit of seeking the will of God. In doing so, we give consent to this basic urge. Without satisfying our craving for direction, we can have no real sense of fulfillment.

After the apostle James tells us that God offers His wisdom to us in all matters (see James 1:5), he then goes on to make a very practical point in verses 6 through 8: "But when you ask him, be sure that you really expect him to tell you, for a doubtful mind will be as unsettled as a wave of the sea that is driven and tossed by the wind; and every decision you then make will be uncertain, as you turn this way, and then that. If you don't ask in faith, don't expect the Lord to give you any solid answer" (TLB).

The Mind of Christ

Don't you long to know what Christ would say about a perplexing situation if He were sitting there with you? How would He approach this problem? What decisions would He make? Wouldn't it be reassuring if your mind just naturally and unconsciously locked into the mind of Christ in all matters, like a radio locks into a transmitter? You would then be

able to function perfectly and consistently in agreement with
His will. What a difference it would make to our lives if we constantly tried to discover God's mind before acting on our own
impulses. We could avoid making fools of ourselves, or worse
yet, getting ourselves into serious trouble.

Does this sound far-fetched? I suppose it does to nonbelievers.
It might even sound a little eerie to think you could be so in touch
with God's mind on human matters or that He could actually have
some immediate influence over your thinking. But isn't this exactly what James is telling us? Is it a pipe dream or a mystical
fantasy? For the believer who understands, it is reality. For everyone else it is foolishness.

An overview of church history reveals that each great leader
in the Christian realm, down through the centuries, took the
time and trouble to seek the mind of Christ. Great saints of God
steeped themselves in Scripture, studied it, and prayed about it
until His Word was carved into their minds. Christ's way of thinking became like a huge canyon, directing their own stream of
thought until there was simply nowhere else for it to go. There
was only one way they could have acted—the canyon was too
deep to allow their thoughts to escape.

"What would Jesus do?" In my experience, when I stop and
ask myself this question, Christ is always there to give me an
answer. He has not left us without a Comforter who "shall teach
you all things, and bring all things to your remembrance, whatsoever I have said unto you" (John 14:26).

As a psychologist, I am greatly impressed by the scriptural
accounts of Christ's thinking. His mind, while on earth, was
extraordinary by human standards, so much so that we are
clearly directed to "Let this mind be in you, which was also in
Christ Jesus" (Phil. 2:5). It is our duty to know the mind of
Christ and, with His help, to emulate it. Reflect with me on the
nature of Christ's mind. In the description given in the second
chapter of Philippians, verses 2 through 9, we are told that
Christ's mind is:

- A loving mind ("having the same love"), v. 2.

- A godly mind ("equal with God"), v. 6.

- A servant's mind ("the form of a servant"), v. 7.

- A humble mind ("he humbled himself"), v. 8.

- An obedient mind ("and became obedient unto death"), v. 8.

- An exalted mind ("God also hath highly exalted him"), v. 9.

If you examine the accounts of Jesus' actions and conversations in the Gospels, you will discover that He exemplified every one of these qualities. He was the perfect example of everything He calls us to be. But what about us? Don't you long to possess these same qualities? I certainly do. And can we live up to these standards? Humanly speaking, no. But with God's help, we can try.

I believe that a Christlike mind can become a habit as natural as breathing. The mind of Christ is God's gift to us, but we must be willing to receive it. Personal attachment to the Lord Jesus Christ and His point of view is one thing a Christian believer cannot neglect.

A Final Admonition

As I conclude my discussion of this tenth and final habit, there is one word of admonition I would like to leave with you. It is very easy to get into the habit of thinking that being a follower of Jesus Christ is a good thing because it holds out so many beneficial consequences. In many ways this is true. But my warning here is that we shouldn't make the benefits of Christian living our primary goal, but the One who is behind them.

We cherish God's wisdom. We bask in the harvest of His words. We delight in prayer. But let me pose this question to your heart, not your head, *Do you seek after God for who He is or for the benefits that come from Him?* This is an essential question, because in these days the Gospel of Christ is being presented as the great lottery of all time. "Come to Christ and be prosperous!" This is the promise being offered to our modern Christian culture. You see it on every Christian television station and hear it in most pulpits of the land. And when God doesn't deliver, disillusioned seekers abandon Him for some other quick-fix, gift-giving visionary.

Thomas à Kempis lived most of his adult life in a monastery where he wrote many works of devotion. None is more famous than *The Imitation of Christ*. Since becoming a Christian in my late teens, I have never been without a copy of this devotional book. *The Imitation of Christ* speaks about being faithful to God, with an emphasis on grace, poverty, and humility. It warns us to guard the senses, including our thinking, against distractions and temptations. One of its most powerful devotions is in the fifty–ninth chapter entitled "All Hope and Trust Are to Be Fixed in God Alone." He writes:

> *What is my greatest comfort among all the things that appear under heaven? Is it not You, O Lord, my God, Whose mercies are without number? Where have I ever faired well but for You? Or how could things go badly when You were present? I had rather be poor for Your sake than rich without You. I prefer rather to wander on the earth with You than to posses heaven without You. Where You are, there is heaven, and where You are not are death and hell.*

Thomas à Kempis is telling us to love God for who He is, not for His benefits, great as they may be. This leaves many of us in a dilemma. How do we separate His benefits from Himself? The answer lies in examining our motives and attitudes. As we lift our eyes off the benefits, we are able to worship God Himself with all our heart. If there are any advantages to be had, we are wise to relegate our craving for them to the back corners of our thinking.

Charles Dickens is one of my favorite novelists. I grew up devouring Dickens and return to him now and then to restore some balance. His stories are full of satire, morals, and principles. He can make me laugh and cry at the same time. His stories are set in the context of tough times and hard circumstances, and this helps me to see my blessings more obviously. Besides, what more entertaining characters can you get than the Artful Dodger, Mr. Fezziwig, and Mr. Micawber?

The plot of Dickens' "Martin Chuzzlewit" is relevant here. It is about a very rich old man whose relatives try to win his favors by groveling at his feet and pledging their undying love for him.

The old man is smart enough to see through their motives and greatly desires to be loved for who he is and not for his money.

One grandson, the younger Martin Chuzzlewit, seems to love him, even though he will not be bullied by the old man. But how is the grandfather to know that the boy can be trusted? He puts the boy to the test. He suspects that the young man is in love with a girl who is the ward of the grandfather, so he sends young Martin off to America where he meets financial ruin. The grandson then returns to England only to find that his grandfather has also apparently become destitute. Despite his own adversity, the young man insists on taking care of them all, including the girl, whom he marries.

Of course the grandfather is not really destitute. But the only way he could confirm that his grandson was worthy to inherit his fortune was to take money out of the picture.

I often wonder how many of us would pass such a test if God decided to withhold His blessings? How long would it be before we would go somewhere else to find a more bounteous god who reinforced us with little gifts so as to keep our fickle love? Without question, we would all fail the test to some degree.

Thomas à Kempis acknowledges that God sometimes exposes him to various temptations and hardships, all for his own good. He then says, "You ought not to be loved or praised less in this trial than if You had filled me with heavenly consolations."

This attitude should not be viewed as a relic of late-medieval piety. It is just as relevant today as it was when it was first written. God deserves our total devotion whether or not He delivers the goods we desire. Our modern minds have difficulty with this, and we desperately need to remedy the distortion. God is not our Great Reinforcer, working some scheme to earn our love. He is the Creator of the universe who deserves our unconditional worship—no matter what. May we be among those who can say with all sincerity, "I had rather be poor for Your sake than rich without You." This is a habit above all habits. Without it, our minds will never achieve true health.

Exercises for Developing Your Thinking Habits

Healthy habits are not a thing of chance but of choice. As with any bad habit, a new and healthier habit can be practiced so as to replace a bad one. By attending to the "stream of thought," it is possible to redirect our thinking into healthier channels. Healthy thought habits also help to eliminate "useless" emotions, those feelings that serve only to punish and rob us of our happiness.

In this section I will lay out practical exercises that can help you shape and practice healthier patterns of thinking. Careful attention to these exercises will not only enhance the mood of your existence but will improve your relationships and chances of success as well. The thoughts we build into our character determine the direction of our lives, as well as their final destination.

CHAPTER 15

CONTROLLING YOUR STREAM OF THOUGHT

Cherish your visions; cherish your ideals;
cherish the music that stirs in your heart,
the beauty that forms in your mind,
the loveliness that drapes your purest thoughts.
James Allen

The activity of your mind is like a stream that flows through your consciousness. In fact, psychologists call this the "stream of thought" because that is exactly what it is. It begins, like a mountain stream, as a spring somewhere out of consciousness. It passes briefly through a narrow window of awareness. Then it moves on again, beyond your consciousness, to influence some other part of your being.

Sometimes it is a small stream—just a trickle. Your mind is quiet, and there is little activity to consume its attention. During those times, your whole being is peaceful and unaroused. Adrenaline is low, daydreaming high. It is as if the mind is in neutral, freewheeling, not engaged in any gear.

At other times the stream is a raging torrent. Thoughts fill your head to the point that you feel it will burst. They scream at you for attention. Thoughts are turbulent and fast-flowing at these times, tumbling over each other and eroding everything in their way. These are periods of high stress, and you are pumping adrenaline like mad. Such episodes are somewhat exciting, because adrenaline is a stimulant, but they are unsettling at the same time. There is no relief even in sleep, because the stream continues to surge into slumberland, feeding dreams with its craziness.

The stream of thought, then, is something we must reckon with. Unless we take control of it, it will take control of us, and it can be a demanding taskmaster. The key to controlling our emotions lies in learning how to have some influence over our stream of thought.

The Source of the Stream

Humans are always thinking. Unlike rain-fed mountain streams in the visible world, the stream of consciousness never dries up. The first issue for us to consider, therefore, is the source of this stream. Where do thoughts come from? Their source is really a mystery, part of the whole self-consciousness phenomenon that all humankind is blessed with. All we really know is that thought emerges some-where outside of our consciousness before it becomes conscious.

This raises an interesting question: Can God influence this stream in some way? Can He cause thoughts to originate under the influence of the Holy Spirit before they become conscious? I've thought about this carefully, and I believe He can. Apart from His Word, how else can God speak to us? We don't hear Him with actual voices from heaven today, because we are living under grace, and He has spoken His last word to humankind through the cross. What we do receive, however, are promptings at the source of our stream of thought.

So, it is quite conceivable that God prompts our thinking. His still, small voice is very much alive today. Of course He doesn't control us directly, since this would jeopardize our free will. When I hear His still small voice prompting me, I can either obey it or ignore it.

And this raises a second interesting question: While God can very well prompt our thoughts at their source, why are we not always open or receptive to the prompting? I believe we are some-times deaf to the voice of God because we don't attend to our stream of thought. John tells us that "the sheep follow him: for they know his voice" (John 10:4). It takes well-tuned spiritual ears to "know" when His voice is prompting our thoughts.

Apart from God's involvement, thoughts don't have to come spontaneously and randomly. To some extent we can all intentionally originate a thought, and we can choose what thoughts we want to originate. Consciously and deliberately, we can begin with an idea and feed it into the stream of our consciousness. It can be any thought we choose. This is an important principle to keep in mind as we consider ways for building a healthier mind.

For instance, suppose I decide to think about my mother. Suddenly I experience a flood of thoughts going back to my childhood. My mother died soon after we first came to the United States, and I doubt that I have consciously thought much about her over this past year. Yet, by my choice, I am now thinking about her. My thoughts flow strongly, so I have to exercise some selectivity, directing where I want them to go. Memories come surging back to me, and each memory presents an array of thought options I can follow, starting a new chain of other thoughts.

Some of my thoughts bring pleasure. Some bring pain. While I can originate some thoughts, from time to time there are others that have their own origin by association, and I can do very little to control them. In fact, the more I resist them, the stronger they may come. We call these "obsessions," especially if they persist even though we decline them. The fountainhead for such thoughts, usually of the unpleasant variety, is out of my reach. I can't switch off the stream of thought. I can only try to influence it by selective attention once it reaches my consciousness.

The one point at which I have control over my thoughts is where the stream passes my awareness. At this point I can reach in, identify a thought, and replace it. I do not need to dwell on what is being presented to me. I can set it aside, even ignore it, and choose something else. In fact, this is the strategy for controlling thoughts that I want to share with you.

Where Do Thoughts Go?

Now we have some insight into the origin of thoughts. But where do they go after they have left our consciousness? Interestingly, one place they go is to the body. In a mysterious way, thoughts become translated into reactions that can cause physical changes in every part of our being. Thoughts can cause stress, fear, anxiety, depression, agitation, irritability, and anger.

While good thoughts are healing to the body, bad thoughts are quite harmful, and they have the power to activate every part of our system. A sour face is not a thing of chance but is a reflection of sour thoughts. An ulcer in the stomach is not accidental. It is a consequence of too many fearful thoughts being allowed to play havoc with our bodies.

To protect our emotions and our bodies, we must guard our minds. We can encourage right thinking by feeding our stream of thought with right thoughts. We are able to discourage wrongful thoughts by changing the beliefs and attitudes that give rise to them. But if we simply ignore thoughts, they end up influencing our bodies.

Paul, in his second epistle to the Corinthians, may have had this idea in mind when he outlined a plan of action for our uncontrolled thoughts. He suggests "bringing into captivity every thought to the obedience of Christ" (2 Cor. 10:5). The New English Bible translates it this way, "we compel every human thought to surrender in obedience to Christ."

I cannot think of a clearer way to summarize the point I am trying to make here. Either we bring our thoughts into captivity, or they will imprison us in sick and troubled bodies and minds. It is better to be captive to Christ's mind than to be hostage to the mind of the world. While we all need help from God to do this, let us not minimize the important role He expects us to play. God will only do what we allow Him to do within us.

Thoughts Create Thoughts

Thoughts not only have their own fountainhead, they can also spawn their own tributaries. This is the reverse of the natural river system, where tributaries feed small rivers until they become larger rivers. In thoughts, large ones give rise to smaller ones that become streams in their own right.

For example, as I sit thinking about my mother, those thoughts bring back many feelings, both happy and sad. Those thoughts then trigger other streams of thought. Some are about my father; others are about my brothers, grandparents, my early childhood, my first day at school, and so on. Thoughts lead to thoughts. And I can't seem to control the "chaining" from one thought to another through the associations they set up.

I used to have a patient who would come into my office, sit down, grin at me, and say, "I've been thinking again!" What she meant was that she had spent many hours dwelling on her thoughts. Invariably, these thinking spells brought her nothing but misery.

Too many thoughts inevitably lead to trouble if we don't know how to handle them. Whenever that particular patient thinks too much, she starts a chain of ideas that can't stop, and she has come to almost fear her thoughts because of the pain they cause. In the following chapters, I will describe some of the exercises I taught her. Her thinking problem is actually quite common, so the exercises are important ones to master. They can help eliminate obsessive patterns.

Changing the Stream of Thought

From what I have described thus far, it should be clear that our thoughts have two main tributaries or sources. The diagram in Figure Three shows these two tributaries. I will consider each in turn and show how we can use them to our advantage.

THE STREAM OF THOUGHT

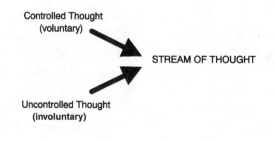

Controlled Thought
(voluntary)

STREAM OF THOUGHT

Uncontrolled Thought
(involuntary)

FIGURE 3

The first source for our stream of thought is voluntary. We can control our thoughts by intentionally originating them. These thoughts do not take us by surprise; we are fully in control of them. We choose and deliberately encourage them, because we are able to think about anything we want at any time we want, including pleasant memories and images of beauty.

Try doing this regularly, especially when something is bothering you: As soon as you are aware of an unpleasant or bothersome thought, reach into your repertoire of experiences and grasp a pleasant thought or memory. Then reflect upon it, drawing yourself back to it again and again whenever your mind strays back to the unpleasant thought.

Controlling Your Thoughts

The second source of the stream of consciousness is uncontrolled thoughts. These thoughts are involuntary, unchosen, and not necessarily welcome. Sometimes they intrude into our awareness like a burglar coming to rob us of our peace of mind. Other times they stay hidden, waiting to attack until they can achieve their damaging effects. As if they have a mind of their own, they intrude at the most inopportune times.

A healthy mind must have the skill to reduce the influence of these uncontrolled thoughts. We do this by making sure they are always out in the open, deliberately keeping them in our conscious awareness. They are easier to control and cannot do the same amount of damage when we are able to stare them straight in the face as they speak to us.

To cope with involuntary thoughts, begin monitoring your thinking on a regular basis. If you have a wristwatch that beeps on the hour, set it for this function. If not, choose some regular event that takes place throughout your day and use it to alert yourself that it is time to "sample" your thinking. For example, assess your thoughts every time the phone rings. Or do it whenever you walk past some particular spot in your home or office.

Every time your watch beeps or you are cued by a familiar activity, stop and ask yourself what you are thinking about. Write down the thought or thoughts on a card or notebook, then decide whether you really want to think that thought. If not, substitute a more acceptable one. This practice forces you to pay closer attention to your stream of consciousness. It also prepares you for the specific exercises that follow, thus increasing your control over both the voluntary and involuntary sources of your stream of thought.

CHAPTER 16

CHANGING YOUR MIND

The weakest soul ... believing this truth—
that strength can only be developed by effort
and practice, will, thus believing, at once
begin to grow divinely strong.
James Allen

I n the previous chapter I described how the stream of thought is formed. Now I will demonstrate the ways in which our thoughts can be changed. Remember this: You can change the way you think. You simply need some direction about how to do it.

As you examine your thought life and take steps to change it, do so with complete dependence on God to give you victory over years of deeply ingrained habits. He longs to help you renew your mind. He wants to bring forth all the hidden and suppressed resources of your being. He wants to elevate and transfigure all the natural talents within you, glorifying them with the gifts of His grace. This is reality.

All God needs is your cooperation, and He will enable you to discover and actualize your deep, real self. Then, as you surrender this self to His grace, you will find that it multiplies like Jesus' miracle of loaves and fishes. You will discover that there is more to your existence than you ever dreamed possible.

Exercises for Controlling the Stream of Thought

There are five basic steps to be followed in taking control of the stream of your thought. These steps are:

1. Thought capturing

2. Thought evaluating

3. Thought challenging

4. Thought changing

5. Thought prevention

I suggest that you learn each single step first before trying to combine it into a sequence. At first, this may seem to require a great deal of concentration, but before long, the steps will follow in easy succession, and you won't even have to pay attention to what you are doing. At that point, your new way of thinking will have become a habit for you—a good habit. Let's go through each of these basic steps one by one.

1. Thought Capturing

All thought control requires that we are first able to capture the stream of our thought. We must know what we are thinking before we can decide whether we want to change it. Two exercises will help you accomplish this. The first is the use of an emotion to reveal the thoughts that triggered it.

The second is the use of bothersome, ruminating thoughts to discover the series of thoughts that preceded them. For both these exercises you will need pen and paper, so have that on hand. A "thought notebook," or a handful of index cards (3 x 5 cards are a convenient size) is very important—you'll want to carry one or the other with you at all times.

Exercise
Purpose: To discover the thought or thoughts that have precipitated a particular emotional reaction.
Step 1: When you realize you are having an emotional reaction, stop for a moment and label the emotion. This forces you to admit that you are feeling something. Write it down, whatever it is. Here are some possibilities:

I am angry.

I am depressed.

I feel guilty.

I feel anxious.

I feel hatred.

This step is important because, as Christians, we don't always want to admit to ourselves that we are feeling negative emotions. Of course, you can also write down positive emotions and help to build your awareness of these.

Step 2: Ask yourself: "Why am I feeling this way?" All emotions, particularly the negative ones, are signals. They are telling you that something is wrong and that action is needed. Write down as many reasons as you can think of.

Step 3: Now ask yourself: "What thoughts led up to my present feeling?" Try to identify the chain of ideas that preceded the emotion. Perhaps someone criticized your work or idea. What did you say to yourself when you became aware of the criticism? Did you say, "I am not appreciated; I never get anything right; I am stupid and nobody loves me"? Write down the thoughts that passed through your mind in the sequence in which they occurred.

Step 4: At the end of the day, take your thought notebook or cards and review all of your entries. Compare them with previous entries. What do they tell you? Examine the reality of what you feel. Reinforce how irrational some of your ideas are and how unnecessary many of your negative feelings are. Once you've completed this exercise, create a pleasant thought to end your day.

Exercise

Purpose: To identify the thoughts preceding an obsessive or ruminating thought.

Step 1: When you realize that you are thinking excessively about some idea or event, write down that idea in a brief sentence that completely communicates the thought. Take note of the time of day and record that, too. Ruminating is like chewing the cud.

The thought goes round and round in your head until you feel quite dizzy. It is likely to keep you awake at night, so this exercise is helpful when you suffer from insomnia. Keep your notebook next to your bed.

Step 2: Ask yourself: "When did this idea start?" Try to pinpoint the event or thought that began it. Perhaps it was a telephone conversation, a letter, or a visit. Briefly describe the event in your notebook.

Step 3: Now consider this: "Why does this idea bother me?" The assumption is that if you have a thought spinning endlessly in your head, it must be something troublesome. Does it threaten you? Anger you? Frighten you? Interfere with your wishes? Cause you to lose control? Write down a brief statement about why you think the idea troubles you.

One word of caution: Sometimes, especially when we are fatigued, ideas will become repetitive and ruminative when there is no real threat in them at all. This is caused by our tiredness and is probably due to a temporary imbalance in our brain chemistry. No doubt you have experienced the feeling of being overtired yet unable to go to sleep. Pay no attention to your thoughts when you are this way. They are not legitimate thoughts. The problem will go away when you have had adequate sleep and when you are rested. If it persists, you need professional help.

Variation: Keep a record of all the thoughts that bother you, no matter how long they last. At the end of a week, review these thoughts and see whether there are any themes that keep occurring. Do certain people always bother you? Are there certain times of the day when you are more bothered than at other times? Does some particular activity always spark a reaction?

By carefully recording and reviewing your reactions over a period of time, you will develop considerable insight into your life environment and your personality style. It will help you to quickly pinpoint where and what you need to change.

2. Thought Evaluating

Now that you have learned to capture your stream of thought, the next step is to evaluate your thoughts. This prepares you to decide whether or not you want to change your thoughts.

Like it or not, we are constantly assessing what goes on around and within us. Unfortunately, although we are not always aware of this, our emotions are largely determined by this evaluation process. Quite unconsciously we ask ourselves many questions, such as: "What did he mean when he said that?" Or, "Why is she looking at me that way—did I do something wrong?" Or, "I know he doesn't believe me—what am I going to do?"

We interpret the thoughts, feelings, and moods of others through their words, tones, inflections, body movements, and facial expressions. We seldom accept things at face value. Our minds seem to be suspicious and distrustful by nature, and our ceaseless evaluations go on without any deliberate intention on our part.

Jesus knew that people do this. Do you remember when He healed the palsied man, with the scribes standing nearby? We read in Matthew 9:4, "And Jesus knowing their thoughts said, Wherefore think ye evil in your hearts?" Jesus wanted people to be aware of what they were thinking and why they were thinking it. How else could He draw attention to hypocrisy and disbelief?

By keeping ourselves alert to what is going on in our minds and by being curious and observant about our thinking, we can avoid the blind spots that characterize unhealthy and unsuccessful people. To know what you are thinking and why you are thinking it is to know yourself. This enlarges the scope of your life by making you open to the richness of all the wisdom of God. You are more in tune with God if you are more in tune with yourself. Thought evaluating is a simple exercise whereby the thoughts you have captured are carefully reviewed and analyzed to determine the following:

- Are these thoughts the real issue?

- Are they based on reality?

- Are they honest?

- Where are they likely to lead to next?

Exercise

Purpose: To carefully analyze a thought and determine whether there is a reason for it and whether the emotion following it is justified.

Step 1: For this exercise you will need your thought note-book or some index cards. Prepare a number of cards or pages as follows:

Thought:

Underlying issues:

Reasons:

Evidence:

Decision:

Step 2: Take a thought you have identified or captured in the preceding exercise and write it next to "Thought" on your card. You may wish to work on three or four thoughts at one time, but don't attempt more than this. Write each thought on a different page. Try to focus on the most troublesome of your thoughts first. The more troublesome the thoughts, the fewer you should try to work on at one time.

Step 3: You will need some thinking time for this step. Go where you cannot be disturbed and prayerfully take each of the thoughts you have written down and consider the following questions:

What is the real issue behind this thought? Is this really what is bothering me or is there a deeper issue?

Ponder your answers for a while before writing anything down. Think about the sequence of events or thoughts leading up to this troublesome thought, and then consider the reasons for it.

Here are some possibilities: "Do I need love? Power? Security? Respect? Reassurance? Am I resisting change? Am I scared? Am I anxious? Is it that I just need an outlet for my feelings?" When you feel you have developed a good understanding of the issues behind your thought, write them down, as briefly as you can, next to "Underlying issues."

Step 4: Then ask yourself: "Is this issue based on reality, or is it imagined? Are you distorting reality?" Be absolutely honest, even if you don't feel like agreeing with yourself. Write down your response next to "Reasons" on your card.

Step 5: Ask yourself: "What is the evidence for my thought? From where did I get this idea? What proof can I give that this is true?"

Let me give you a model for using Step 5. Suppose you have just been criticized by a friend for not doing him a favor. You feel depressed because of the rejection your friend's comments imply. As you examine your thoughts, you identify one main theme: "I am a worthless person unless I can please my friends at all times." The underlying issue behind this thought is your general feeling of low self-esteem and your need always to be winning the approval of others by pleasing them.

You then ask yourself: "What is the evidence I have that if I please others and do what they want me to do, I will be a worthwhile person?" As you ponder this question it should become obvious to you that there is no evidence that you will be a better person. Pleasing others only sets you up for more rejection because if you do not go on pleasing them they will be even more upset. If you please them sometimes, they will expect you to please them always.

So write down on your card, under "Evidence": "There is no evidence to prove that I am a better person just because I do what others expect me to do. My self-worth is not determined by pleasing others but by God's unconditional acceptance of me."

Step 6: Ask yourself: "What decision should I therefore make? Shall I decide to accept the thought and put up with the associated feeling of unworthiness, or shall I reject it?"

Write your answer under "Decision." In our model, the decision should be: "I will not allow the rejection of others (when I don't please them) to determine how I value myself. I am a worthwhile person, whether or not others value me, because God values me."

Step 7: Having concluded the evaluation of your thought, keep the card or page in an easily accessible place. Several times each day, take out the card and review the response given to each question. Affirm yourself with these responses. Say to yourself: "God, I believe this to be true. Help me to live my life as if it were true."

Variation: This exercise can also be carried out with the help of a trusted friend or as a small-group exercise. Each person identifies a thought and evaluates it as I have demonstrated. The responses are then shared with another person or with the group, who are asked to agree or disagree with the response. The discussion should then both clarify thinking and drive home the truthfulness of each conclusion. The card can then be used for review and for periodically affirming yourself.

3. Thought Challenging

Having captured and evaluated a thought, the third step is that of "challenging" or disputing the thought. This process is particularly important when a thought resists rational analysis, or when the evidence for the thought is ambiguous.

For instance, let's suppose you were late for a dinner engagement and your host has criticized you for "always being late." You may very well have been late because you dilly-dallied while dressing or because you stopped to visit an old friend. In other words, yes, you are guilty of being late. You failed to keep a promise for reasons you could have avoided, so you apologize.

Your host accepts your apology. But you continue to feel guilty. You don't like yourself for being inconsiderate. You've done this many times before, and you fear that this tendency may be deeply ingrained in your personality. No one else is blaming you. Nobody else is punishing you for your error. You are doing it to yourself What do you do now? The next exercise should help you.

Exercise

Purpose: To remove the incapacitating consequences of a particular thought by challenging the underlying beliefs or assumptions of the thought.

Step 1: Select a thought that is bothering you. If you are upset, but don't know why, use this exercise to work backward to identify the thoughts that led up to your feeling. Let's say that the thought goes something like this: I should feel guilty if I do not do what others expect me to do. This is a very common thought, especially if you are accustomed to being a victim.

Step 2: Ask yourself: "Is this thought rational or irrational?" By rational, I mean is there a valid reason for the thought? Are you really guilty or do you just feel guilty? If you are in doubt, call the idea irrational and proceed with the next step. Labeling your thought as irrational when it is irrational helps to drive home the point that reality is being distorted and truth hidden.

If you can honestly say that the idea is rational, sensible, and quite logical, then give yourself permission to experience whatever you are feeling. Feeling guilty when you are guilty is necessary and normal. Feeling guilty when you are not guilty is stupid. In the example above, we must label the thought as irrational. It does not make sense that you should feel guilty when you don't do what others expect you to do.

Feelings that follow rational thoughts are necessary and appropriate. If you are guilty about something, then let yourself feel guilty. Accept the guilt as normal. Just make sure that you feel an appropriate amount of guilt and that it does not last too long.

How long should you feel guilty? Only long enough to seek forgiveness from the one you have harmed and from God. This may involve making restitution. Once you have received forgiveness, the feeling of guilt has served its purpose and should be disposed of quickly. If you continue feeling guilty, you are perpetuating the feeling through inappropriate "self-talk." (More about this later.)

Step 3: If the thought is irrational, then proceed to challenge the thought. Challenging is a way of conversing with yourself in such a way that you bring into question the truthfulness (or reality) of the thought. Some psychologists call it "disputing" and see it as a way of changing the underlying beliefs that cause the thought. You fight unreality with reason. You force yourself to ask, "Is this reality?" God has given us reasoning power for this very purpose.

The best way to challenge your irrational thoughts is to do it in writing. Take a thought and write it at the top of a sheet of paper. Divide the paper into two vertical halves. On the left side enter reasons why the thought is true. On the right, enter the reasons why it is not.

The following questions may help you:

- Who says it is true?

- Is there a law that says this?

- Why should I believe this?

- Is this a hangover from childish reasoning?

- What is the worst consequence I can expect even if this is true?

- What prevents me from changing this belief?

- Are there ways I can prove or disprove this thought?

- If I take the idea to its extreme, what is its ultimate conclusion?

Write down all your answers and reinforce the points you are making. Debate with yourself as if you were a lawyer. Convince yourself that, if you insist on getting at the truth in your thinking, you can change your irrational ideas. Trust God to give you His Holy Spirit to convince you of the truth.

Variation: This exercise can also be carried out in dialogue with another, or it can be used as a small-group exercise where each member of the group is given an opportunity to work through the challenging of a thought.

4. Thought Changing

Changing a thought can be accomplished in one of three ways. The first method is to repeat to yourself, as often as possible, a new thought to replace the old. For instance, you can write the new thought on a card. Every hour, take it out and repeat the thought to yourself. Slowly you will come to believe it. Repetition in self-talk will change your thoughts. It certainly works when we say negative things to ourselves all the time, so there is no reason why it shouldn't work when we say positive things.

The second method is simply to decide what it is you want to believe and then believe it. This is not as hard as it may seem. If the previous exercise of challenging an irrational belief is effective, you should be so convinced that you can change your belief without any further ado. I've watched many of my patients do this, and I've done it many times myself. When you are convinced, you change your mind.

Not everyone finds this to be easy. If you cannot easily change your thought, no matter how overwhelming the evidence for the change is, the third alternative is to see a counselor or psychotherapist. Your thought patterns may be too deeply ingrained to respond to self–help. This is particularly important if the thought pattern was formed during your early–childhood period. You will not be able to use reason, evidence, or facts to change your beliefs that easily.

5. Thought Preventing

Just as the body can be exercised to increase its resistance to disease, so can the mind be exercised to increase its resistance to unhealthy thoughts or emotions. Prevention is better than cure, and this is as true in the realm of our emotions as it is in our bodies.

Rather than waiting for an emotional or thought problem to arise, you can rehearse your reality thinking during your sane moments. You can probably conceive of a number of ways to do this. Rather than providing step–by–step instructions for a specific exercise, I will outline some general principles and leave you to use your own creativity.

Exercise

Purpose: To teach oneself to think more rationally during times of normal emotion and to practice healthy thinking.

Action: Prepare a list of your unique and commonly used irrational ideas, then play a game with yourself. See how many rational counterstatements you can devise for each irrational thought. Write your personalized responses on cards and keep them with you for frequent reviewing. Use Scripture wherever you can to support your rational counterstatements. This will help you to develop the habit of rational thinking so that it can be used spontaneously when a real–life situation occurs.

Variation: You could set up a system whereby you reward yourself for each new rational counterthought or argument you create. Give points for each idea and treat yourself to some mi-nor luxury when you have reached a predetermined goal.

There is another important aspect to healthy thinking that needs to be addressed. It is our tendency as humans to think by talking to ourselves, and it is known as self-talk or "self-conversation." Self-talk is a powerful controller of our emotions and behaviors. It is so important, in fact, that I will devote the next chapter to a discussion of how you can take control of your self-talk.

CHAPTER 17

How to Change Your Self-Talk

Self-talk changes the picture—it changes the
programming, which creates the belief,
which develops the attitude, which creates
the feelings, which controls the behavior.
If you'd like your child to do the right things . . .
Start with his or her self-talk.
Shad Helmstetter. Ph.D.
What to Say When You Talk to Yourself

My grandmother loved talking to herself, and I mean talking out loud. And her habit has rubbed off on me. I was about eight or nine years of age when I first noticed it. My younger brother and I would stay with our grandparents every school holiday in their large home located on the Vaal River in South Africa.

In the evenings I sat with my grandmother at the large dining-room table. As she crocheted, I watched and listened. Sooner or later she would start talking to herself. She called it thinking out loud. I was fascinated by her habit, and only much later in my life did I come to realize how healthy it was.

Let me hasten to reassure you that my grandmother wasn't eccentric or strange. In fact she was a very sane, devout Christian who taught us about salvation, sanctification, and "being good boys." But she had this thing about talking to herself whenever something was bothering her. She said it helped to clear her head of "mice who build nests when you aren't looking and eat up all your happiness."

Whenever she was angry, she would sort of reason back and forth, first taking one side, then the other. Soon the anger was

173

gone. She would find a reason to give it up and convince herself that being angry served no purpose. I watched her lose her anger right before my eyes. If she was planning a new project or organizing a trip, I'd hear about it as she talked to herself. She really didn't mind my eavesdropping. In fact, she said it made it better to have someone listen in on her self-conversations. My grandfather was a little deaf, so there was no fun in speaking her mind to him.

I picked up on my grandmother's ideas about self-talk later in my life, during my late teens. It wasn't the thinking out loud that first caught my attention. What I discovered was the value of speaking out loud anything I wanted to memorize. I was studying to be a civil engineer at the time, and that meant examinations of endless formulas and facts.

One Saturday afternoon, as I was studying, I asked Kathleen (then my fiancée) if I could read to her from a textbook. At first she protested, saying she wouldn't understand any of it, but finally she relented. I made a most remarkable discovery— everything I read to her stuck with me. She didn't have to understand it or even pay attention to it. Just speaking it aloud helped to fix it in my mind. I have continued this practice ever since.

This illustrates a type of self-talk that can powerfully change your mind. My grandmother's idea that one should speak out loud what he or she is thinking is right on target. If you don't externalize your self-talk, you cannot capture it or modify it. This chapter, then, is about capturing your self-talk so that you can use it to create a healthier way of thinking. I will lay out several exercises that should be practiced regularly until they become habitual.

Understanding Self-Talk

Before we proceed with these exercises, however, I need to explain self-talk. My grandmother's talking out loud is only one form of it. A lot of self-talk is silent, which is why it is so dangerous. The key to turning self-talk to our advantage lies in periodically speaking out or writing down what we are saying to ourselves. Self-talk takes on a new meaning when we do this. If you try it, you'll see what I mean.

Many psychologists, especially those who use cognitive strategies, emphasize that much of our thinking takes place in the form of conversations we have with ourselves. We literally talk to ourselves all the time. This self-talk generates ideas that ultimately become translated into emotions. Since our reasoning is carried on as a conversation, you would think we could be aware of the content of the conversations. Unfortunately, unless we attend to our self-talk, we are often unaware.

Furthermore, self-talk is usually more irrational and illogical than conversations with others. We think more clearly when we talk to someone else than when we talk to ourselves. Often, when we share our feelings and thinking with someone else, we "see the light" and have a better understanding of what is happening to us. Suddenly, everything makes sense, and we realize how ridiculous our reasoning has been. We can become more aware of our thinking by learning how to eavesdrop on our own self-conversations. We can then counter any disturbing ideas in a rational and logical manner.

Let us suppose you have just had a conversation with a friend. Your friend has told you that she does not want to go to dinner with you next week. She is sorry she has had to cancel this engagement, but something has come up. As you go back to your office, you begin to converse with yourself. The conversation may go something like this:

"I wonder why she doesn't want to go to dinner with me? She knows I planned this weeks ago. She knows how much I have looked forward to it. I wonder if her mother has been talking to her. I know her mother doesn't like me! What could her mother have said? Perhaps I didn't show enough enthusiasm over her garden, but would she hold something like that against me? Maybe I shouldn't have called so late the other evening . . ."

Before long, you're saying, "Nothing ever goes right for me. Ever since I can remember, things have gone wrong. Life is terrible to me. I must be jinxed or something . . ." Before long, you are deeply depressed, even though none of your thoughts are true.

Explore Your Self-Talk

Does the previous self-conversation sound ridiculous? Why don't you try writing down every conversation you have with yourself regarding your spouse, kids, boss, employees, pastor, or friends and see how ridiculous some of your self-conversations sound. You'll be surprised at the sorts of things you say to yourself. It isn't until we see our thoughts written out that the irrationality becomes obvious. Think about the following characteristics of destructive self-talk:

- Self-talk tends to be emotionally charged. It comes from hurts (real or supposed) and is fed by other feelings.

- Self-talk is fueled by a vivid imagination. It seldom stays in touch with reality. It exaggerates and oversensitizes us.

- Self-talk overgeneralizes. It takes one minor event and tries to make it explain a constellation of other circumstances.

- Self-talk is irrational and illogical most of the time. It feeds off doubts and uncertainties and is seldom satisfied with reality.

- Self-talk usually leads to a "catastrophizing" of everything. It always ends, as my fictitious example does, with statements like "I am jinxed," or "I am terrible," or "Nobody cares for me."

- Self-talk is usually self-pitying and selfish. You are the center of the conversation and the focus of everything, and you want to wallow in your mire and lick your wounds.

Those realities should ready you for some exercises in what is perhaps the most important habit of all—learning how to change your self-talk. Healthy and successful people are able to recognize and stop their negative self-talk. They can analyze its content and arguments, set aside the ridiculous and imagined, test reality, and take whatever action is necessary. They know how to inject healthier and more realistic ideas into their self-conversation. This keeps them from being influenced by evil thoughts.

Here is an exercise to help you monitor your self-talk.

Monitoring Your Self-Talk

Exercise

Purpose: To help you become aware of the conversations you have with yourself, especially those that are illogical and irrational.

Step 1: Set an alarm or use some device to signal you at least once every hour. You can use class breaks, coffee breaks, or any other natural break in your day to signal the time for the exercise.

Step 2: At the moment you are signaled, stop what you are doing and review very carefully the conversation you have been having with yourself during the previous five minutes. Write it down as sentences. Try to recall as many ideas or self-statements as possible. Pay particular attention to the conversation you are having with yourself at the moment the signal occurs.

Step 3: Take your list of self-talk sentences and review each one. Ask yourself the following questions about them:

- Is it true?

- How do I know it is true?

- Is it reality?

- Am I overreacting?

- Will it be different tomorrow?

- Am I being sensible and realistic?

- What's the real issue?

- Where will this idea take me?

Step 4: Deliberately counter your negative self-talk with positive, realistic, reassuring sentences. For example, say to yourself, "It is unfortunate that this has happened to me, but it is not the end." Or, "Who says I have to be this way? I'm being irrational and illogical, and therefore I will not pay attention to what I am thinking."

Step 5: Find someone (a friend or spouse) to share your thoughts with. Irrational self-talk is best challenged in open conversation with another person.

Variation: You can monitor your self-talk at any time. Once you know how to do it when cued by set times, try catching your self-conversations at random times during the day. Monitor your self-talk while you are having a conversation with a friend or while standing in line at the supermarket. The point is, increase your awareness of what you say to yourself.

Changing Old Self-Talk Habits

While the exercises I have described are fairly straightforward, you may find them difficult to perform. Old habits die hard. Many years of irrational self-talk are difficult to eradicate. Don't lose heart if you don't change quickly! Nothing worthwhile is achieved without cost, so be patient and persistent. Master one step at a time.

It is especially helpful to pray about your self-talk. God is interested in how you think and wants to renew your mind. You are not alone in your efforts!

Exercise

Purpose: Teaching yourself new "mind games" to improve your rational thinking.

Action: We learn many negative and self-destructive mind games in life and few positive ones. Define negative mind games as patterns of fixed responses to situations in which the "rules" are predetermined, well rehearsed, and continue indefinitely unless you do something to stop them.

In this exercise I will describe a series of negative mind games and then suggest positive alternatives. You may be able to design some positive mind games that fit your personal needs. Try your hand at this. You may be surprised at how creative you can be.

What you say to yourself determines your feelings and behavior. A common negative mind game is saying the most ridiculous things to yourself and not realizing how ridiculous they are! If you are being irritated, say, by a neighbor's barking dog, as I was recently, don't say to yourself, "I can't stand it! That noise is driving me crazy." Saying this to yourself doesn't remove the irritation; it merely prescribes how you are going to feel.

The truth is that you can stand it, and it will not drive you crazy. Learn to speak the truth to yourself. A more honest alternative is to say, "That dog's barking is very irritating to me. I will call the neighbor and ask him to take care of the dog." Such a self-statement brings change. It specifies the action that is to be taken.

Similarly, don't say to yourself, "I can't do it," or "Things should be better," or "This is going to hurt me." These statements become self-fulfilling prophecies. Learn to recognize them and substitute healthier and more truthful alternatives.

Watch the derogatory labels you put on yourself. Another common negative mind game is convincing yourself that you are humble by labeling yourself in a derogatory way. "Oh, I'm just stupid," or "I'm so paranoid. Don't pay any attention to me." These labels are defense mechanisms. You're afraid others will think this way about you, so you jump in first to avoid the pain of finding out what they think.

Again, these become self-fulfilling prophecies. They are not honest, and they distort reality. Always label your feelings correctly. Don't say, "I am stupid," but rather "I'm sorry; I made a mistake. I will try to do better next time." Don't say, "I am paranoid (schizophrenic, getting old and senile, or any other derogatory label)." Say, "I tend to worry easily," or "I'm not looking at things realistically." A healthy self-attitude can never exist if you label yourself in a derogatory manner.

Watch the derogatory labels others put on you. There are people who accept, without challenge, the labels others put on them. If someone of influence says, "You're stupid," agreeing with the statement may be your way of avoiding further conflict. Worse yet, you may even believe it's true.

Don't do it! Receive such labels with gracious repudiation. Refuse to accept the general descriptions others place on you. If a spouse says, "You always do this to me," remind him or her that *always* means every time without exception. This can only mean he or she is exaggerating, so you cannot accept the statement as valid. There must be at least one exception that makes such a statement untrue! If he or she can't see the contradiction then he or she has the problem, not you.

There are two important things to remember about name-calling: The first is that it is always used as a weapon to punish; the second is that words are only symbols. They derive their power from the meaning we attach to them. Words are simply representations, yet we irrationally and unrealistically respond to them as if they were real in themselves. In fact, we can choose whether or not to allow them to hurt us.

Whatever you do, don't form the habit of hurting back with words of your own. Jesus has taken all the questionable fun out of revenge! Gone is the superficial pleasure of seeing others cringe at our venomous name–calling. In its place He has given us some simple rules:

> But I say unto you, Love your enemies, bless them that curse you, do good to them that hate you, and pray for them which despitefully use you, and persecute you; That ye may be the children of your Father which is in heaven. (Matt. 5:44–45a)

Eliminating Useless Emotions

Another important application of healthy self-talk habits is that they can be used to eliminate our "useless" emotions and enhance the necessary ones. Golda Meir, the former Israeli prime minister, once said: "I have always felt sorry for people afraid of feeling, . . . who are unable to weep with their whole heart. Because those who do not know how to weep do not know how to laugh either."

These are great words of wisdom spoken by a woman of strength and leadership. On the other hand, Charles Dickens once wrote, "There are strings in the human heart that had better not be vibrated."

Who is right? Both, of course.

Throughout this book I have tried hard to advocate a balance between staying in control of one's unnecessary emotions and enhancing the necessary ones. In other words, we should be free to feel whatever we are feeling yet be selective in what emotions we entertain. Pitiful is the state of anyone who goes to either extreme.

Ever since the early days of Sigmund Freud we have been told that our emotions are dark secrets created by unconscious and mysterious forces over which we have no control. Even worse, we've come to believe that our emotions are so obscure and hidden from us that we don't even know what we are feeling. Frightening, isn't it? Only if you assume it's true.

In recent years there has been a dramatic change in the way psychologists view emotion. After almost a century of believing that emotions were mysterious and beyond our control, we have rediscovered that they are not all that baffling. They are simply the end product of what we think. I say *rediscovered* because this truth has really been known for a long time.

Prior to the advent of modern "depth" psychology, most philosophers had figured out the connection between thoughts and emotions. Frankly, many of the early psychologists made it more complicated than it is. Today, however, psychology is gradually coming to accept the fact that our thoughts are the real culprits, not other mysterious, secret, and unfathomable goings–on. Imagine that—you feel what you think. And all the time Scripture has been saying, "For as he thinketh in his heart, so is he" (Prov. 23:7).

Which Emotions Cannot Be Controlled?

Many painful emotions are quite beyond voluntary control. Some are caused by biological factors. If, for example, I am feeling depressed at the same time that I have the flu, I probably am experiencing an emotion that is a symptom of an underlying illness. To cure the emotion I have to cure the illness. It is normal that we should experience these emotions, because they are protective signals that must be heeded.

Furthermore, our feelings are not simply in our heads. They are the consequence of many complicated electrical, biochemical, and other changes in many parts of our body. Parts of the brain, the endocrine system, and even the state of tension in our muscles all contribute to our emotional experiences.

While our biological states are often affected by what we think, it is also possible for a part of our body to be diseased or dysfunctional. This, and only this, may be the cause of a challenging emotional state. The healthiest thing we can do with these states is to accept them and seek the right medical treatment.

But normal feelings are a different story. These are the result of what goes on in our thinking, and we literally create or eradicate them a thousand times every day without even knowing what is going on in our thoughts.

Where Is Your Treasure?

Emotions are the consequence of the meanings (or beliefs) we attach to events, not of the events themselves. I believe this idea is thoroughly biblical. The Gospel places great emphasis on the value we place on certain things. In the Sermon on the Mount, Jesus reminds us of this when He says, "Lay not up for yourselves treasures upon earth . . . But lay up for yourselves treasures in heaven . . . For where your treasure is, there will your heart be also" (Matt. 6:19–21).

Scripture often equates the heart with the mind. In effect, Jesus is telling us that what we value will determine who we are, how we think, what we say to ourselves, what gets our attention, and how we feel. These verses are then followed, in the same chapter, by a series of commands about how we should think:

- "Take no thought for your life" (v. 25).

- "Which of you by taking thought . . . ?" (v. 27).

- "Why take ye thought for raiment?" (v. 28).

- "Therefore take no thought" (v. 31).

- "Take therefore no thought for the morrow" (v. 34).

These are all commands against the type of thinking we call worrying, which can better be translated "anxious thought." Of all the painful emotions we are all prone to, anxious worrying must surely be the most common. Clearly, anxiety is fed by the way we think. Somewhere along the way, we have learned how to think in a worrisome way.

Healthy thinking is a way out of this pain. To think healthily may be fear provoking, but fear is easier to deal with than anxiety. Fear is tangible; anxiety is vague and intangible. Successful people cannot afford to spend too much time in "worry pain." It saps energy and detracts from more important things.

Thoughts and Emotions

It is very easy to demonstrate to yourself how feelings can be created by thinking, especially by the conversations you have with yourself in your mind. Go for a walk and recall some meaningful early-childhood experiences. Talk to yourself about them for a while. Try to recall all the details. Then stop and note what you are feeling. How did you feel when you started your walk? What are you feeling now? The change is entirely due to your thinking.

Or, think of an old friend (better not make it a current one) and begin to recall all the negative things about him or her you can remember. Think about those unpleasant traits for a while. Very soon you will start feeling all sorts of negative emotions—anger, hatred, or disgust, depending on the history of experiences with your friend. These will be due entirely to your thinking.

Now, stop thinking about the negative experiences and start to recall all the positive things you can remember about your friend. Continue to think about them for a while. Soon your feelings will become positive again. You are likely to feel warm, loving, and friendly toward your friend.

Try this exercise a few times until you are convinced that you can create or remove your feelings by what you think.

Feelings Follow Beliefs

The cognitive approach to psychotherapy emphasizes that every emotional reaction is the inevitable consequence of our beliefs and attitudes. Emotions are not the consequences of any particular action or event.

For instance, if a friend tells you she hates you, you are likely to become very upset. You will feel miserable. But it will not be the words of your friend that will cause you to feel this way. The message may be the trigger for what follows, but your consequent feeling will actually be created by what you believe and by how you think about the message. It is because you expect to be liked by your friend that the rejection bothers you. If the same message came from someone you knew to be an enemy, your expectation would be different, and so would your feelings.

This is where psychological actions are different from physical actions. In the physical realm, if you slap me I will hurt. The slap is the direct cause of my hurt. In the psychological realm, words are only symbols—they do not hurt directly. Verbal slaps must have meaning attached to them, or else they do no harm. It is the meaning we attach to words, based on our beliefs, attitudes, expectations, and assumptions, that gives them the power to create emotions in us.

This is both good news and bad news. The bad news is that psychological hurt is not as easy to avoid as physical hurt. After all, you can always run away from someone who wants to hit you. The good news is that since psychological hurt is mainly caused by words, we can easily learn how to minimize or avoid hurt altogether. It is just a matter of attaching new meanings to the words that bother us.

Conclusion

We've come to the end of this book. I hope you've learned a few important principles and have been inspired to become a healthier thinker. Perhaps you have been challenged to look at some familiar ideas in new ways. After all, that is what learning is all about.

This raises one final challenge I would like to leave with you. The illiterate individual of the future will not be the person who does not know how to read but the person who does not know how to think. I have tried to show how deficient our thinking is in the realm of the emotions.

We are imposing on our minds the same burdens we have inflicted on our stomachs—precooked ideas. Our talk is at the level of the lowest common denominator. Predigested ideas at the lowest price is the diet of our age, marketed by "McThought." And it is sad for me to say this, but Christian thinking has deteriorated along with the rest of our culture. The Christian mind has virtually lost its capacity to digest a healthy, robust meal of good and healthy ideas. It wants sound-byte suggestions, instantaneous cures, and easy solutions.

Little of what I have presented here falls into the "instant cure" category. All these ideas require attention to detail and commitment to work. However, I do believe that with the Holy Spirit to help us and with a little directional change, we can revolutionize our thoughts. I believe we can create wholesome attitudes and thus learn to live more fulfilling and meaningful lives. I hope and pray that this book inspires you to transform your mental habits and to develop a healthy, godly mind.

Chapter 4

1. Marcus Aurelius, *Meditations* (New York: Washington Square Press, 1964), 70.
2. Stephen Covey, *The Seven Habits of Highly Effective People* (New York: Simon and Schuster, 1990).
3. *The American Psychological Association Monitor*, July 1995, 50.

Chapter 11

1. Tori De Angelis, *The American Psychological Association Monitor*, November 1988, 22.
2. "'Learned Optimism' Yields Health Benefits," *The American Psychological Association Monitor*, October 1995, 10.